DATE DUE

Connecticut Author

The Man in the Cell

by

Wayne Michael O'Connor

Copyright © 2012 by Wayne Micheal O'Connor

The Man in the Cell
by Wayne Micheal O'Connor

Printed in the United States of America

ISBN 9781619963290

Unless otherwise indicated, Bible quotations are taken from New International Version of the Bible. Copyright © 1985, 1995, 2002 by The Zondervan Corporation.

www.xulonpress.com

Table of Contents

In the humble hope that even one
person will come to trust in our
Lord Jesus Christ.

To my wife Karen

The Man in the Cell

Chapter 1

"Hey you!" Archarius called into the small dank cell where the haggard and bloodied man sat crumpled in a heap. "You there," Archarius called again; the man in the cell with his long hair soiled with sweat, dirt and blood slowly lifted up his head and turned toward Archarius, revealing a swollen and beaten face. As the man turned his head, his eyes caught Archarius' and for only a moment, Archarius became unsteady on his feet; he stepped back with just his right foot, subconsciously improving his stance to one of power and strength. Archarius' hand dropped to his sword and he grasped the cold hilt in his fingers. Withdrawing his sword barely an inch out of its sheath, his eyes still locked on the stranger's, Archarius waited for the man's response to his command, but the man remained silent and said nothing. Archarius stood in front of the cell as if ready to defend himself against this helpless man, who would struggle to stand if ordered and who sat locked behind iron bars. He struggled with why he suddenly seemed insecure and remembered his original intent; he shoved the small filthy dish of spoiled food in under the bars.

Finally, with what seemed like a look of disappointment, the man turned away and once more hung his head, his hair again hiding his face.

This particular cell had been designed large as it was built to hold many men. They had all been moved out and relocated elsewhere to make room for this prisoner, this apparently dangerous prisoner who warranted his own guard. The large cell was dark, beyond filthy and the air hung heavy with dampness. Large stone blocks formed two sides of the walls as well as the floor and the ceiling. The other two sides of the cell held iron bars with only one entrance, including a small slot to slide food into the prisoners. The only light to be seen emitted from the burning torches that were hung on the walls of the corridor. This large corner cell occupied the end of the stone corridor. Placed opposite the cell and against the wall lay a wooden stool and an oaken barrel of water designated for the guard. A smaller far less fresh barrel of water sat next to it for the prisoners. In this damp and uncomfortable setting is where Archarius would spend the next twelve hours. His shift had barely begun and he dreaded the long night lying before him. Archarius was not aware of the identity of the man in the cell or even why he was being held here or why he had been treated so brutally. Nevertheless, this man stood to be tonight's assignment; tomorrow would bring another prisoner as this man was to be brought before the court in the morning and the prisoners rarely came back here after that. Somehow, his instinct told him tonight would be somehow different. Perhaps a rescue attempt would be made by this man's friends or perhaps even an offered bribe from a friendly official. Anything could happen, but the question remained, what would happen? He did not know the answer, but he did sense that he had become uneasy and this awakened him from his boredom. As the night began and the first few hours were uneventful, he recognized himself starting to relax and because of the relaxation in his body, his mind began to wander.

Chapter 2

Caius Petronius Archarius thought back to his first year as a recruit and the reputation the family name of Petronius held, the name was one of honor and one of courage. This family name had opened the early doors for him as he joined the army at the age of nineteen. But in the ranks, he is known as simply Archarius and the name suited him well as he could be his own man. He remembered the excitement of receiving the seventy-five denarii after he swore his oath and his allegiance to the Emperor. He had just barely made the requirements to join the Roman Army. Although he met the height requirement of five feet and eight inches, his frame at that time had been a slight one and seemed almost to sag under the weight of his shield and sword. His superiors noticed this shortcoming and promptly assigned him the simple and menial tasks in camp. He became angry and troubled by these assignments at first, as his place and status in the barracks reflected this low rung of assignment. The simple assignments soon appeared much more palatable when he witnessed the main group returning from their latest march of twenty-five miles, dusty, hungry and exhausted. After years of childhood visions of grandeur of being a Roman soldier, he grew quite disappointed and disillusioned by his life in the barracks. He had envisioned hearing about the past battles and the glory won through victory. He wanted to hear all the wondrous tales about the exotic parts of the empire and beyond that the traveling Roman soldiers had experienced. Instead, he saw the corruption as his fellow recruits bribed the Centurion's deputy to avoid any of the loathsome tasks that were required to maintain the barracks. Instead of stories of glory, Archarius found gambling and the subsequent arguing that almost always followed. There did, however, exist many good and well skilled soldiers in the legion. Sadly, the group he met and had been exposed to consisted of just average men looking for a way to profit and pass the time between the campaigns. They were definitely not the heroes of his dreams.

The barracks themselves were not much better than the hallways he now patrolled beneath the palace. His squad had been assigned two small rooms. The first room consisted of their living quarters and also for sleeping while the second room had been designated to house all the equipment for the eight men in his squad. Their room lacked even a window as it had been built up against another row of rooms. Out their front door lay a long colonnade which provided their only source of fresh air and light. Time spent in the small cramped room remained restricted only for sleeping as even the dust and the hot sun outside usually made for a more inviting environment.

Archarius soon became well thought of within the ranks; he had shown himself to be bright, he liked to learn and more importantly, he liked to listen. A trait rarely found among men in general, not to mention soldiers. He studied his fellow soldiers, their reactions to adversity as much as their reaction to the mundane. He became an astute observer of men. As the years went by, Archarius grew, matured and became a seasoned soldier; yet in his mind he remained still the same inquisitive youth who grew more and more disillusioned with his present way of life. He could, like others, turn on the switch which would transform him into a brutal and efficient fighter, but afterwards he would return to his other self, the questioning and searching soul. Archarius grew to be a frustrated and tormented man. It seemed as though several men lived inside of his body, the soldier and the brute, the thinker and the poet and finally the judge or the counselor. To which personality did he truly belong? When with the soldiers he acted as one of them; when with men of knowledge, he was inquisitive and when faced with conflict, he became the regulator. All these types of men existed inside of him, but none could claim to be the man himself. He wondered if other men were also struggling internally and would this always be his misfortune. He hated the confusion this torment caused, for he thought himself weak and undisciplined because of these thoughts. There must be one true self; there must be one that is the dominant trait, there just had to be.

So far in his career the tales of his battles sounded far less interesting or as terrifying as the stories of his fathers. Archarius' tales of glory are limited to disbanding small groups of rebels while traveling from one trouble spot to another. The years of service by his father held far more exciting tales. The elder Petronius became involved in trying to recapture the area lost to the Germania tribe after the horrible and embarrassing defeat at the Battle of the Teutoburg Forest. It was there, under Publius Quinctilius Varus that three legions of Roman soldiers died at the hands of the Germanic warriors. Varus had been deceived by a Germanic tribal leader named Arminius who had made an alliance with Rome. Varus foolishly allowed himself to be swayed into altering his route and thus walked straight into an ambush. The Romans were not in their combat formation and the marching line of soldiers had foolishly stretched out an incredible nine miles. This left both their flanks horribly exposed. The Romans were now strung out too far, and to worsen the situation, the infantry had become separated from the Calvary. This forced the Romans to fight many small battles, all from a point of underdogs as the Germanic warriors held the higher ground and had more advantageous weapons and this ultimately proved them victorious. This loss had effectively stopped the expansion of the Roman Empire throughout Germania until the armies that included Archarius' father invaded the area again; this time, however, with burning revenge in their hearts. Correcting the errors of the past and not underestimating their adversary, they succeeded after just a few small skirmishes to reoccupy the land that had been lost as well as to gain additional territory. His father's legions had returned to Rome in glorious triumph.

Archarius was, of course, thrilled when his father returned home from a campaign, but there were other reasons for his joy. Due to his father's position in the army, many times other soldiers would come to Archarius' house to speak with his father in regard to either previous or upcoming campaigns. The men would gather in one of the outlying rooms and speak in hushed tones as they dissected the recent performance of other leaders within the legion. Archarius would stay hidden in the shadows, listening to every word and trying to picture the events as they took place based on the narratives he had heard from the stories.

Most discussions would be on strategy or specific performances by individuals, but it was when the men began to describe the battles that caused Archarius' heart to beat so fast, he had to restrain his breathing as to not give away his position. The stunning descriptions of the violence and the bloodshed both excited him and frightened him at the same time. To be so close to an enemy when it was obvious that one of you would live and one of you would die was somewhere Archarius could not envision himself. How would he respond to such finality, such a pivotal moment where the very next movement or thought may well be your last? The stories of looking into a man's eyes as he felt the thrust of your sword into his body and knew, indeed, his time had come would be chilling to a man, but it created terror for a boy listening and hiding in the shadows. The stories of the severed limbs and the endless streams of blood which would begin to flow downhill as the battle intensified created pictures in his mind like none before. These were the stories that both thrilled and terrified young Archarius.

How did his father thrive in these kinds of situations, yet sit calmly at the family dinner table, wink at his wife and inquire to how Archarius' studies were progressing? Had his father become mad or were all men like this? Would Archarius be like this also one day? Would he be one moment standing up to his ankles in blood, with death all around him only to be at the family dinner table that Sunday without an adverse effect? Archarius knew not what the future held for him nor did he know what kind of man he would be, but he wondered if other boys or even other men had these observations, these thoughts of conflict or were these thoughts the cornerstones of what kind of man he would become?

When Archarius grew bored and complained of his studies and had asked that his father tell him stories instead about his campaigns, his father would remind him, any man can swing a sword or throw a spear, but to lead men in battle required study, focus and training. Archarius' father had always been a thinking soldier, one who planned objectives over and over until he was confident that he had planned for every contingency. This is how his father wanted Archarius to approach everything in life, as a campaign to end only in victory, no matter the objective. Archarius understood this vision and believed in it, but he secretly doubted his ability to be so bold and so wise.

Chapter 3

Archarius' passion of observation caused him to take particular notice of the man in the cell. This strange man did not fit the annoyingly predictable pattern of the typical prisoner. Archarius had been offered bribes many times by prisoners whose families would make him a wealthy man, if he would only unlock the cell and turn his back, if for only a moment. Just a moment of his time and he would be a very wealthy man. He had never been sure if he had turned down these bribes out of loyalty to the Emperor or out of the fear that if he were caught, his punishment would be worse than that of the man whom he had let escape. The other constant angle used by the prisoners would be to attempt to appeal to his heart and his sense of family. "I have children and a wife," they would cry out to him. "They will perish without me." Archarius never let on, but this tempted him much more than the promise of wealth. He saw what happened to the families of convicted prisoners. They were shunned and eventually driven out of the city, left to try to survive in another town where they knew no one. But again, his loyalty or his fear, which one had prevented him from acting?

This man, however, concerned Archarius as well as he interested him. He obviously was important enough in someone's eyes to warrant his own guard but usually the men this important were not beaten like a slave. This man truly had enemies and this made Archarius even more nervous because there would doubtlessly be attempts behind the scenes to help him if he was this important and yet treated this badly. He began to pace the corridor nervously, alternating watchful glances toward both the prisoner and the exit. This was going to be a long night and this time, not because of its boredom.

Archarius had a bad habit since adolescence of sighing. The sighing functioned mainly as a catalyst to try to calm his emotions. This routine of sighing did not fit in well with the common practices of a Roman soldier and Archarius had endured much ridicule for this habit in the past. But tonight as he paced the corridor, he let out a lengthy sigh, one filled with exasperation and futility. As the sigh left his lips and the air left his lungs he turned around to find the man in the cell was staring straight at him. The man didn't say anything nor did he appear to be amused by this odd behavior by one of Rome's famous soldiers. He just looked at Archarius with a very odd expression. Archarius couldn't put a name on the expression shown on this man's face, but it seemed forged almost of concern. Archarius turned away and proceeded down the corridor to get a drink of water out of the oaken barrel. As he nervously drank the water, he wished, instead, he was out walking in the morning sunlight and this man was no longer his responsibility.

Chapter 4

Daydreaming is and always has been an integral part of guard duty. The only way to not only look alert, but to also survive the endless boredom of guard duty was to allow the mind freedom to wander. This had always come easy to Archarius. Since his boyhood, his daydreaming served as his escape from fear and hurt and now as a man, a needed respite from the doldrums and worries of life. In his youth, he impressed and often amazed himself by his own imagination. He could just shut his eyes and actually watch the events unfold like a play right in front of him with characters he did not know and actions of which he could not predict the outcome. He once foolishly asked his mother why he could just shut his eyes and see such an endless parade of vivid escapades. He hoped it to be a gift or perhaps a blessing from one of the gods. He can still remember the sting of embarrassment and disappointment when his mother replied, "That is just your imagination, and everyone has one, you know." Still, he thought, his must be better; surely, no one else has such a vivid one.

He used his imagination now, closing his eyes while he sat on the stool in the dark corner of the corridor, his ears alert for any footsteps announcing a unexpected visitor or an inspecting Centurion. He relaxed and tried not to think of the dank, foul place he sat in, but instead allowed his mind to take him out into the sun on a pleasant summer day. He saw a dusty road turning into a road of smooth marble with fig trees lining the sides shading the marble which felt cool on his unsandaled feet. He heard the far away sounds of children calling to each other and as his head turned, he noticed the clouds spinning effortlessly around the outline of the sun. He walked with tireless legs and sensed his surroundings more than he saw them, the smells of the olive trees, the sounds of the insects and the wind rustling the branches ever so slightly. It was truly a beautiful moment and he finally felt peaceful. He sighed, slowly but loud enough that it awoke him out of his daydream. He slowly opened his eyes and the sadness of his reality again filled his eyes, mind and heart. He threw his cup back into the water barrel and continued his pacing of the corridor.

As he walked down the dimly lit corridor, he stopped momentarily, trying to bring back that feeling of peace that he had experienced in his daydream. But his eyes were open and they were filled with the signs of quite another feeling, one of pain, of suffering and of fear. He had grown immune to this place, immune to the screaming, the sobbing and the bloodshed. What kind of a man was he that he could calmly walk down these corridors where you could almost taste the anguish? This horrible place existed and he was indeed part of it. Every morning as he left and walked out into the daylight, he felt the guilt lay over him like a shadow as he tried to shake off the visions and the thoughts of what he had seen that night. He knew that though he now walked in the warmth of the sun and his hunger now satisfied as he had eaten, from where he had come was immense tragedy and great suffering that was left behind to fester until his return. Surely he thought the battlefields were worse than this, but why was he so affected by these tortured souls? He sat down on his stool and thought about the words he had just used--tortured souls. This suffering and agony was destroying their bodies but what about their souls? What would the gods do with these miserable people? Would there be more agony in store, greater than any agony he or they could possibly imagine? What about him? Life seemed difficult for him but what of the after-life? How would the gods receive him? What of his sins? How angry had he made the gods with his indifference? Did the gods even know or care about him? Suddenly, Archarius felt cold and unsettled. He detested when he let his mind run away from him like this. Sometimes this mood and sense of dread would follow him for days; yet other times, it would slowly fade away. These thoughts always tormented him; even when he was far removed from the dungeons, they clung to him like a filth that he could never cleanse himself of.

This assignment surely affected him much more than any campaign he had fought in, but why, why did it plague him so? As he walked past his post in front of the prisoner's cell, he said aloud without meaning to, "Oh, to just have a peaceful life." "If you believe, you will receive whatever you ask for in prayer" (1). The sound of another voice in the dark startled him. The man in the cell now stood upright. His body remained twisted and battered, but his face seemed almost serene, strangely lit by warm and passionate eyes. For a moment, it was not a guard and a prisoner looking at each other but two men looking at each other's eyes, one with curiosity and one with pity, but it was not the guard whose eyes revealed the pity.

Archarius made it a point never to speak with prisoners except to issue commands. He didn't want to become familiar with them, he didn't want to hear their crimes or their excuses, and he didn't want to learn about their families; in fact, he didn't want to know them at all. He turned away from the man, walked back to the corner and sat down on his stool. He stared at the man, another priest he thought, one who became too outspoken and insulted the wrong person. This one did seem different though, as he showed no fear or no sense of panic like most in his situation.

The man in the cell went back to the rear wall of the cell and sat down, his legs slightly bent with his feet flat on the floor. His hands rested on his lap and his head tilted back to the wall so that his face pointed up to the ceiling and he closed his eyes.

What had he said, Archarius thought to himself, "If you believe"; then like a child who cannot hold his tongue, "Believe in what?" Archarius heard his own words at the same time he realized he was speaking. He drew in a quick breath as if to take back his words, but his effort came too late. The man in the cell did not turn to look at him, but slowly a smile came to his badly swollen lips.

Chapter 5

Archarius was familiar with the gods as they were part of the daily life of the citizens of Rome, but involvement occurred less frequently among the regular soldiers. He personally found the numerous gods and deities confusing. Although he had taken part in the festivals and joined in the dedications to Jupiter and Cocidius, he had remained mainly a spectator. Truthfully, he simply didn't feel any sense of interaction in his life on behalf of the gods and whichever god this man in the cell was referring to, he was sure it, too, would be equally ineffective in improving his life. *There were so many gods*, Archarius thought, *that the heavens must be crowded with them.* The priests maintained that the many successes of Rome were due to the favor of the gods. Archarius thought it had more to do with the Roman legions than the gods. He was sure the enemy had their gods as well, but against a charging cavalry followed by the thunder of ten thousand footsteps, he doubted their prayers had much of a chance. He chose not to share these irreverent thoughts with others, as he did not wish to be on the other side of the bars that he now guarded.

This man's words of worship were strange, for they reflected good fortune back toward the worshipper instead of gifts directed to the gods. It had seemed to Archarius, most gods simply wanted endless sacrifices. He stopped himself and considered why he was even reflecting on this man's words.

As if the man in the cell had heard his very question, he again spoke, "I am the bread of life. He who comes to me will never go hungry and he who believes in me will never be thirsty"(2). The man never opened his eyes or even turned his head as he said those words; he just sat with his back against the wall.

Archarius stared at him for a moment and then reluctantly took the bait. "What is your name?" asked Archarius. "You must be a priest, but you speak as if you think you are something more." The man said nothing nor even acknowledged that Archarius had said anything. Just as Archarius began to become angry, the man stood up and looked at him and smiled. The man then said with an air of calmness, "I am the Son from whom the Father has sent to save you and all men." Archarius became disgusted and frustrated that he had let this prisoner get to him and that he was unable to just dismiss him. He stood up quickly and kicked his stool up against the man's cell. It hit the iron bars and skidded down the corridor. The man in the cell shook his head slowly, sat back down and again closed his eyes, one of which was beginning to shut permanently from the swelling. Archarius walked the length of the corridor and grudgingly retrieved his stool and threw it back in the corner where it belonged.

Soon after, a guard patrolling the palace came by under orders to check that no attempts have been made to free the prisoner. Seeing all as it should be, the guard started to leave when Archarius stopped him and nodded toward the prisoner. "Do you know who this is and why is he so important? If I am to ensure that he is here for the morning, I should be aware of his identity." The guard pointed at the man in the cell and sneered, "His name is Jesus of Nazareth; he claims to be the King of the Jews and a great prophet; he doesn't look too powerful right now though, does he?" The guard laughed, slapped Archarius on the back and walked away.

Archarius, like most Romans, was not fond of the Jews as he thought their claim to be the chosen people of their god displayed their arrogance. The Jews were also intolerant of Roman customs; while Rome allowed many different religious sects to gather in the city, the Jews would accommodate none but their own. The title King of the Jews was not one that instilled awe or even respect to most Roman citizens. As for the prophet characterization, that would explain the cryptic and confusing prayers he had heard. *Kings, prophets, priests, too much of what we don't need,* Archarius thought, *these people only complicated things; most proved to be corrupt or a fraud in the end.* Rome needed a strong hand to guide her but one who also had compassion for the trials of its citizens. These were hard times and there were many obstacles in the way of individual success or even a long life. Archarius knew he was different from the other guards to think these thoughts and have disparaging opinions of Rome and of life in general. The attitude of the average Roman soldier was first, to stay alive and second, to gather as much glory and, of course, money as possible.

Archarius sat back on the stool and faced the cell that held this Prophet King. What had this man said earlier? Hungry and then satisfied, he had said, satisfied how, he wondered?

Hungry, for what Archarius thought to himself, "What will be given to me that I will be satisfied?" He spoke the question out loud, but he had a tone to his voice he did not intend to include, but his next question came out even more harshly: "Where is your army, if you are a King? Why do they not rescue their King?" The man in the cell did not answer nor even look at him or acknowledge he had heard a word that Archarius had spoken to him.

The next few words that Archarius had uttered shocked him and he quickly looked around to ensure no one else other than the man in the cell had heard them. "I'm sorry, I did not mean to sound so cruel," Archarius said softly. The man in the cell shifted slightly and turned his head to look at Archarius, "You are forgiven" was all the man said in reply to Archarius' apology. The irony of this conversation was not lost on Archarius, or the odd feeling of comfort he sensed when the man looked at him and said the words, "You are forgiven." Who is this man and why did Archarius have a need to be forgiven for his rudeness? Those eyes of his, it was those eyes; in them he saw hurt, judgment and forgiveness all visible to him in just a glance.

He wanted to ask another question, but wanted to make amends for his rudeness so he asked, "what should I call you? What is your name?" The man in the cell slowly and painfully stood and faced him and said, "There are many names, but you may call me Teacher as I am here to instruct you so that you will hunger no more."

As Archarius stood near this man, he began to sense his maturity slipping away and with it, all the pretenses, facades and arrogance that comprise an adult. He remembered what it was like to be innocently inquisitive again, to feel before he thought so his opinions would originate from the heart and not the molded adult perspective. He felt time slowing down and he felt less of the physical sensation of his muscles and his armor and more in the sensations of his senses, listening, seeing and feeling. The walls he had built so long ago, the walls that shielded him from the callousness and disappointment of the world, the walls that he had built up throughout his life were suddenly fading away, leaving just his true self without all its complications.

With this naked awareness, there came flooding back wave after wave of memories. Visions of his childhood, games he had played, things he had seen, people he had loved. His mind was racing and it ignored the present as it focused on sending Archarius further back in time. All this was overwhelming him. He saw his formative years, his awkwardness, his misguided passions and the friends he had long since forgotten. Now he was seen as a young man, as his journey came to a sudden halt at one specific and vividly clear memory, a time he had shared with his father by the river Jordan.

Chapter 6

Several years before he became a soldier, Archarius traveled along the Jordan River, just south of the Sea of Galilee with his father. They had stopped for food and drink and sat upon a large rock situated between the trees at the bend of the river. In the distance he could see a small group of people gathered along the river's edge. He could see them fairly well, yet he remained out of range of their voices. He noticed it to be an odd group of people. The group consisted of travelers, some who appeared quite poor, properly dressed men and even a few soldiers. This odd group stood at the edge of the river listening and speaking with a man who looked unkempt, poorly dressed and acting very strangely. Archarius thought that he actually may have been mad and these people were trying to settle him down. The odd man stood just a little ways out into the water which seemed to be about waist deep and appeared to be speaking to the group while all the time wildly waving his arms. At first he thought one of the group had begun to fight with this madman as he saw the strange looking man forcing the other under the water. The second man was let up just seconds later and appeared surprisingly grateful to the strange man and not upset with him at all. Then one at a time another and then another member of the group would walk out to this strange man, only to be put under the water. After getting out of the water, they would be embraced by the others on the shore and then together they would walk away. *What a strange sight,* he remembered saying to himself. His father had been attending to the animals during this time and had paid no attention to this unusual event at all. He thought of asking his father about this, but decided against it, for his father often considered Archarius uneducated in the ways of the world and he didn't want to embarrass himself further in the event that this was just a common custom that was just not familiar to him.

Weeks later while listening to news being told to his father, Archarius heard of this strange man again. The madman, as Archarius learned, was named John and he was a priest of some sort who walked a very dangerous and desperate path, according to the men who spoke with his father. The madman was outspoken and strong in his words and often criticized important people. His father's friends said that the madman would undoubtedly be arrested someday and executed for his treasonous behavior. Archarius agreed with this, but he still wondered about the odd ceremony in the river. Those other people seemed to be his friends, so this man was not alone in his opinions. But still, men who were too boisterous in their criticisms were often found to be missing one morning. Archarius' curiosity continued as he remembered the strange ritual in the water. Would he ever understand the purpose or learn of the fate of any of the people whom he saw in that group?

Chapter 7

A rcharius opened his eyes, only to take in the terribly depressing environment of the dungeon that had replaced his idyllic place on the riverbed. Another guard on his rounds had commented that this man John had known the man in the cell and supposedly regarded him as a greater priest than he. The fate of this John had not been known to him, but Archarius felt sure it would end badly. Archarius shook his head as he considered that there were just too many people believing too many things, too many cultures, and just too much nonsense. Many gods existed in the Roman culture, yet few knew much about them, not to mention what the gods themselves expected from their subjects. He secretly wondered what difference they really made in his life at all. However, Archarius kept these thoughts buried deep within his mind, as he still feared the wrath of an angry or slighted god. In his travels throughout the city and the countryside, he had seen the many altars built to Jupiter, Apollo, Diana and many more; some had even built altars to gods he was not familiar with or even heard of and he had considered himself educated in these things. Even within his unit there were groups of soldiers who would stop before and after a battle to build an altar in tribute to one of the gods. He had taken part in some of the group dedications but to this point, he had not personally orchestrated any particular testament.

Archarius now looked over at the man in the cell; he still sat in the same position, his eyes closed and surprisingly a slight sign of a smile shown upon his face. This man looked physically weak; likely, even when healthy before the beatings, he probably did not pose much of a physical threat; certainly he had never been trained to fight. Jesus of Nazareth -- that is what the other guard had informed him. Archarius had heard of the town of Nazareth. A small town, more like a village really, filled with masons and carpenters all involved in rebuilding the nearby capital of Sepphoris. A peasant village, not a town seemed to be the better description for Nazareth. From a village such as this came this prophet, this King of the Jews?

It all seemed very unlikely that this man in the cell would be considered so dangerous to the state. The catalyst surely is that this man must have caused someone high up to be very irritated or he would not be held here with a guard assigned to watch over him until his trial.

Standing to stretch his legs, Archarius walked back and forth in the corridor; how he hated assignments like this one. He wanted to be out in the field, traveling throughout the country. Traveling with the Roman army proved to be the most exhilarating thing he had ever been part of. He enjoyed the constant vigilance that was needed as they had often traveled into unfriendly towns. The few battles that Archarius had been part of were not even true battles in the normal sense. They were more like skirmishes against poorly coordinated mobs from these strange cities. He admitted to enjoying seeing the fear that the approach of his unit caused and he remained confident in his training, as he should be, for he possessed honed skills in fighting. Surprise and sometimes superior numbers remained the only advantages these groups possessed against the Romans. However, these people were not soldiers; they had inferior weapons and were often poorly organized. The fighting lasted briefly; the only part that bothered him was the involvement of the women and older children. They would often support the men of their city by throwing stones from the rooftops or from behind walls. Archarius would pursue and kill the men who threatened him, but he never gave chase to the others. It seemed to him dishonorable; however, if confronted directly he would disperse them savagely. Weakness and hesitation were traits never to be exhibited by a Roman soldier.

There were, however, times of quiet when his mind left the brutal realm of his surroundings and became muddled with inner conflict. Should not the focus be on life and its obvious rewards and certainly not taking these very things from so many others? These words were treasonous and perhaps even cowardly, spoken by a soldier, yet he did not believe so. With each year of his growth, he became more and more conflicted with these thoughts. *Rome*, Archarius mumbled to himself, *it is heralded as the center of life, of civilization and of law.* This he agreed with as he had seen the life and camps of the barbarians. They had not the laws nor the arts nor even the wonderfully constructed buildings that existed in Rome. Yet, in the midst of this civilization, there remained brutality, treachery and corruption. Who is he to have these thoughts and opinions? Certainly he was not meant to even to speak to these issues. He had not the education, the family status or even the ambition to entice others to consider his words and what then about the gods? What did they think of Rome, its accomplishments and its failures? Fear cautioned him to even debate these issues in his own mind. He had little daily thought regarding the gods as did some of his fellow soldiers and even some of his friends. There seemed to be so many and in his ignorance, he questioned, shouldn't one god be in charge? Where do they live; do they communicate with each other? Do they know of or even like each other? Did they really care about him? Did they only reward those who made offerings to them?

Yes, these questions were dangerous ones and he trusted no one, not even his own family with which to share these thoughts. Usually at the end of these episodes of internal struggle, he would chide himself for not being worthy of such deep thinking and finally forcing himself back to reality, he slipped back to the routine life of which he was accustomed.

Chapter 8

The sixth hour of the night (midnight) had arrived and Archarius despised the next six hours as he had no idea how fast or slow time was passing until the dawn. There were no water clocks down here in the filthy tunnels, just a man's instincts to mark the hours. Stiffness in his joints and his thirst were his best measures of time here in the darkness of the underground tunnels.

His own thirst reminded him that he was overdue to give water to the prisoner; odd that this man had not even once asked or more accurately begged for water as did most of the prisoners. Archarius filled the mangled metal cup with water and carried it over to the prisoner he had been assigned to guard this lonely evening. He stopped in front of the bars and stared at the man still sitting with his back against the wall, eyes closed and his face pointed up to the ceiling. He appeared more like a man waiting for an appointment than a trial. A trial thought Archarius where the likely decision to end this man's life would soon take place. The blood had stopped in most of the man's wounds, but he could see that the swelling was becoming much worse.

Large contusions began to appear over much of
his body and about his head. Oddly though, his
face suffered far less than his body. One eye began
to swell badly and the forehead was starting to
show signs of bruising but the skin seemed intact.
The same could not be said for his chest and back
where large and ugly gashes had turned into bloody
gaps in the skin due to sections of flesh ripped out
by the scourging. Archarius had seen the weapons
used for these beatings and wondered how this man
could even be alive after being subjected to such
a beating. Perhaps, Archarius considered, due to
his professed title, his face had been left fairly uns-
carred. Archarius spoke loudly but not in anger as he
said "water" and stood before the cell. There was no
response from the man in the cell. Archarius did not
become angry or impatient as his own wandering
thoughts had mellowed his mood. "Water," he said.
"It looks like you could use some." The man rose
and with great effort walked toward Archarius and
stretched out his hands for the cup. He drank slowly
and thankfully. The man raised his eyes upward
and said, "Thank you, Father" and handed the cup
back to Archarius. Archarius became irritated at
this and said, "I'm the one you should thank, as
I brought you the water." As he turned away, the
man spoke, "Give thanks in all circumstances, for
this is God's will for you" (3). Archarius stopped and
turned as he remained irritated. "Do you also give
thanks for the beating you just took and the cell
you now find yourself in?" The reply was quiet,
yet sure, "Give thanks for all things, as this is the
will of God." Becoming a bit sarcastic and ready to
debate, Archarius replied, "Then I suppose you have
angered your God for him to treat you so severely."

Smugly, he turned to head back to his stool when the man replied, "It is the will of God that the Son of Man must be delivered into the hands of sinful men, be crucified and on the third day, be raised again" (4). Archarius turned slowly and faced the man in the cell. He hesitated before he spoke. *Son of man,* he thought, *crucified and then apparently escaping after just three days.* "I don't understand," he heard himself say. "I do not know who you are, I do not know why you anger so many people and I especially do not know why you make me feel so uneasy." The man in the cell started to turn away when Archarius said, "Wait!" Archarius could not see the man's face as it turned away, but a slight smile formed on the bloody, swollen and cracked lips. Jesus turned and looked at the man as a father would look at his child. Archarius, embarrassed by his lack of confidence, paced back and forth and sputtered, "Time passes very slowly here in the tunnels at night. Tell me about yourself so that the night will pass more easily." Again a smile came to those same swollen lips and Jesus said, Sit and we shall talk."

Chapter 9

Still standing in front of the cell, Archarius spoke first, "With all the pain you must be in and especially with the worry of what tomorrow will bring, how can you sit here so peacefully?" Jesus replied, "God has said: never will I leave you, never will I forsake you" (5). Jesus suddenly stopped talking and when Archarius started to ask another question, he was interrupted by the voice of the Principalis "If the Centurion catches you speaking so amicably with this criminal, you may end up joining him in that cell. This man is rumored to be a powerful priest of ways outside Roman law; be careful he does not lure you into his trap." Archarius looked to Jesus to hear of his denial, but Jesus said nothing as if he had not even heard the other soldier at all. "I do not fear this man," Archarius said to the Principalis. "You do not need to fear him, but you need to be wary of his tongue and his magic; perhaps I should transfer you for the remainder of the night," said the Principalis. "I shall speak to the Centurion and move you away from this priest, for your own good." And with that, the Principalis turned and walked away.

Archarius felt surprisingly disappointed. "I am sorry to go, for I have many questions for you." "Do you want to leave here?" asked Jesus. "No," Archarius said, "I feel like..." he hesitated, "I feel like I need to talk to you." "You are strange to me, but I feel as if you may indeed have answers to some of my questions, and I was curious to hear your answers before it's too late and they take you away." "Then do not worry," Jesus said calmly, "for we shall not be bothered for the remainder of my time here." "But the Principalis will surely speak to the Centurion and..." Jesus stopped him in mid-sentence. "Even now," Jesus said, "the man forgets his mission." For indeed at that moment, the Principalis was walking outside in the night air to report to the Centurion that all was well in the tunnels. There was no reported mention of a transfer and no talk of a conversation between a guard and a prisoner.

Chapter 10

Archarius remembered and thought back to when, as a young boy, he had asked many questions and listened to his father trying to understand the things of the world he could not yet comprehend. His childhood had been one of difficulty; neither parent spent much time with him as his father being a soldier traveled often and his mother spent the day trading in the marketplace. Archarius typically found himself on his own for much of the day and so he chose to venture outside the city rather than stay in the heat, the crowd and the dust. He most often visited the forest north of the city. It wasn't a true forest, as it occupied only a small parcel of land, but to a young boy, it proved to be a wilderness.

There were hills, valleys, caves and a small river which snaked itself through the forest. He always visited here alone, never bringing a friend as he preferred to explore by himself. In those days, Archarius taught himself an appreciation of nature. He studied everything he saw: the plants, the rocks and especially the trees. Trees had always held some special appeal for

Archarius. He had been told by a teacher once, some trees are hundreds of years old, and this realization fascinated Archarius. He loved to look at an old tree and wonder what things in the past occurred nearby or had been seen by this tree in all its years. It seemed to him that trees were living history. He identified trees first by their bark and also by their leaves. The beech tree by far became his favorite; with its smooth bark and thick strong trunks, it always caught his eye. He would sit underneath a tree, looking up at its spreading branches and see the blue sky framed by the green leaves. He felt so small when he looked up into the canopy of the tallest trees. It was these moments that nurtured his humility and understanding of the many creations in the world and how very small was his simple part. He swam and fished in the river and built dams to create small pools where he would clear the bed bottom by removing all the large rocks, leaving a sandy bottom and clear still water. Yet the most exciting days occurred when he found a new cave which had been used as a shelter by others long ago. He never found more than the remnants of a fire pit or perhaps a partially concealed wall at the entrance, but he enjoyed imagining who could have occupied this site and how long ago. Had they been fellow Romans or perhaps, he excitedly thought, an enemy camp?

These early years formulated Archarius' individuality and he avoided becoming just one of the mobs as he called them, people whose opinions were formulated by the group and often by the loudest members of the group. Individuality is not the healthiest trait for a Roman citizen, at least not a soldier. Freedom of thought and speech to that degree was best reserved for the Senate floor, not the barracks. Alone on his adventures in the forest, he became free to think about any subject and develop his opinions to any degree and with this freedom came curiosity and an appreciation for things not yet understood.

These days formed his aptitude for considering questions seemingly too deep or too big for a young boy. When did the gods create all this? Had all the creations been accomplished at one time? Did the world always look like it did now? Which gods were first and did they work together to create the world? Why, after all this creation, did they disappear never to show themselves to men or even occupy the world that they had created? He had been mostly confused by the sheer number of gods; there were literally gods for almost every part of nature, the customs of men and their attributes as well as their failings such as a god of jealousy or the god of strife. To him, the seemingly endless array of gods had been positioned as such to take the responsibility for man's failings. Even at his young age, he harbored doubts that all these gods really were present or active in these events. The more gods he knew of, the less scary or extraordinary they appeared to him. Even at this young age, Archarius began searching for something more real. Something that would be more concerned with his life than a multitude of gods whose only involvement was to receive sacrifices and altars.

As he grew older, these doubts intensified but also as his maturity and wisdom grew, Archarius knew enough to keep these thoughts to himself.

Roman law did not prohibit ignoring the gods, but the practice angered many as the citizens predicted the anger of the gods themselves would be visited on the general population. He had learned this lesson in his late teens, when he had made the grievous error of opening up his heart regarding these thoughts to the girl he was involve with at that time. This, indeed, proved to be a decision he lived to regret.

Chapter 11

She had been named Herennia and although she came from an elevated family, it was not high enough for her taste. Beautiful and manipulative, Herennia made a point of catching the eye of whom she pursued. She had set her sights on Archarius and with them as always, a plan. At seventeen, Archarius cared little about Herennia's secret agendas in life; he could not get past her beauty and he easily fell into her web. His family was one of rank as his father had done well and achieved a rank of Decurion and had the leadership of a Cavalry group. Thus, the romance between Archarius and Herennia had been born, the boy looking to satisfy his lust and the girl looking to improve her position. In the short time they were together, they used each other, she to only such a degree as necessary and he providing introductions and acquaintances.

It began on an evening when they were alone out in the courtyard and Archarius had drunk excessively of wine. Archarius began to speak from his heart, a result of the wine, as normally he was quite cautious as to what he said and especially to whom he said it. He spoke of his searching for a purpose in his life and his frustration with the gods and his doubts to some of their existence and also his doubts of their dedication to the average Roman citizen. What had they done for anyone, where does one see the fruits of their blessings? Archarius went on in a rant, detailing the enormity of the number of them. It certainly seemed to him like the gods were a selfish lot, always asking for sacrifices or proof of man's desire and loyalty to them but returned very little to man at all. With each continuing swallow of wine, his comments grew bolder and more dangerous; the alcohol had removed his internal defenses. He did not notice any shock or disappointment on the face of Herennia as he expressed these views, but soon her plans of how to use his outspokenness against him would be clear. Herennia, seeing a chance to gain notoriety and playing the role of a concerned citizen, went to the Centurion to advise him of the poor respect and lack of dedication that his soldiers showed to the gods. When challenged on this point and after more people became involved in the dispute, Herennia presented Archarius' name and his opinions and went further to say that undoubtedly, this lack of worship would be shared by his family as well and who's to say how deep this attitude ran in the ranks of the army? Herennia's smile as she spat out these last words was hard to restrain as she knew that her plan seemed to be working perfectly.

Herennia's claim heard by too many people could prove to be an embarrassment for the Centurion. However, not one that he felt in the mood to investigate so he called his assistant Lucius Rufius Tullis to handle this suspected threat of blasphemy. His assistant's rank, Optio ad Spem Ordines, meant not only was he the Centurion's deputy, but he also was in position to fill the next vacancy of Centurion. This added urgency for recognition to an already impatient and manipulative man. Tullis quickly saw an opportunity to increase the recognition of his name by elevating the case of the blasphemous soldier to the highest level that would hear the complaint. He immediately sent word for Herennia to meet with him to share what she knew. He planned to add embellishments into her story and entice her to include these in her testimony. When these two manipulative people met, their conversation resembled two snakes in one nest, both trying to get the upper hand for their own purpose. Herennia, no longer the innocent and beautiful girl that Archarius had known, for now her true personality laid exposed and the ugliness of her deception and conspiracy had erased her beauty. They both talked and listened, each trying to figure the other's strategy. Herennia easily saw through Tullis' poor attempt at charm and identified him as the manipulator she knew him to be. Finally, seeing the chance she had waited for to improve her status and get involved with a Centurion and perhaps a Tribunal, she confronted Tullis with her frank and calculated agenda and suggested that they could both benefit from this soon to be very public case. Tullis was caught off guard, as he usually had the role of the one suggesting a deal or collaboration. But this girl was hardened for her young years and crafty enough for him to be very careful with or he, too, may find himself in front of a Tribunal.

Their plan was simple. Archarius would be charged with Blasphemy and trying to incite among his fellow soldiers rebellion against the gods and, of course, Rome. Herennia would be the chief witness and Tullis, with supporting testimony from conveniently bought witnesses, would present the case to the Tribunal. They would cry out in the marketplace that the army was full of godless men and how could the average citizen feel safe that the army would not one day turn on Rome itself? These kinds of accusations would bring swift resolution from those in charge so as not to lose the citizens support for the army. Archarius would be killed or punished, it really did not matter to Tullis and Herennia, as they would either be paid off or instead, receive envied and desired positions. Herennia was thrilled at the momentum that her plan had taken, but the sly smile would soon be removed from her pretty face. Word of their deceptive plan leaked out from their false witnesses who ended up betraying them for additional rewards by identifying their true purpose.

Those in power who did not even want the hint of this disgrace in their midst, especially not among the army regulars, decided to take matters into their own hands. They considered among themselves, what if this man, this Roman soldier, was actually worshipping the god of the Jews? This had to be handled quickly and quietly. Archarius had been summoned as well as Tullis and Herennia, but all were to be interviewed at different locations. Upon questioning, it was determined that Archarius did not believe in the god of the Jews. He was found to be just a confused young man and he would be punished lightly for his lack of judgment. Tullis and Herennia were found to be the more dangerous, as their two plans were obviously to embarrass the army for their own gain. By order of the Tribunal, Tullis received a reduction in rank and a transfer to a far less comfortable province and Herennia's father was summoned and told to send his daughter out and away from the city of Rome.

Archarius never saw Herennia again, as her father had been so incensed that she had yet again found herself in another embarrassing and dangerous dispute. He sent her away to live with relatives well out of the reach of important Roman ears. Archarius had no idea of the plot laid by Herennia and Tullis and the danger he was in until years later when it was told to him by a friend of his father.

Chapter 12

All of these memories, as well as the lessons that had been learned, came back to him as he sat on the floor considering what the Principalis could have heard and what the consequences would have been for him. He had avoided serious punishment years ago, but his superiors would undoubtedly bring up the past if yet another situation arose with regard to disrespect of the gods as the subject of the complaint. Unsettled, he stood up and looked at Jesus who had already stood up and turned away. Archarius' head hurt, his cheeks felt hot and his neck felt tense. Since he could remember, these symptoms had always been present when he felt frustrated and confused. It started back in childhood when he had attended school and occurred when he could not understand a lesson the teacher had explained to the class. It had been a mixture of frustration, anger and confusion. He grew frustrated that he did not simply understand the lesson, he was angry that he was not more educated and he became confused by the conflicting thoughts racing through his mind. How had he gotten to this point? Why now could these feelings of frustration and confusion be caused by this prisoner in the cell? All of this confusion because of a man who displayed a peaceful demeanor when he should be frightened for his life?

This man, this prisoner who had actually offered to teach him! Why didn't he just throw a bucket of water on this man to show who is behind the bars and who is in front? It seemed all very odd to Archarius, this man's eyes, his voice, his very presence, they all seem to have an odd effect on him; it stripped away the confidence and the armor Archarius had built up in his mind that protected him all these years. Archarius rubbed his calloused hands over his face, drank the tepid water from the barrel and splashed water on his face, trying to awaken from this mist of confusion he now found himself in. Something was happening to him and he did not like it. No, he did not like it at all. Something seemed wrong indeed and it was happening much too fast for his comfort. His knew that for either good or bad what had started as a simple night of guard duty would prove to be anything but simple.

Chapter 13

Archarius sat back purposely and defiantly on his stool in the corner by the water barrel. He stared into the water as he dipped his cup again, filled it with water and again leaned back against the wall. He sat there sipping the lukewarm water. He reflected on the strange things that had occurred this evening and how odd he himself was feeling tonight. *Obviously,* he determined, *this man is the cause of my uneasiness; in him, therefore, must be the answer. I must continue to question him to determine if he is mad, or perhaps I am mad to be listening to him.* Standing up, Archarius walked over to the cell of the man, leaned against the bars and said suddenly, "I want to talk to you." Jesus stayed where he was, his back against the wall, his face looking up at the ceiling. Just as Archarius was wondering if he would even respond, Jesus said, "The time has come, the kingdom of God is near. Repent and believe the good news" (6). "What is this good news you speak of?" Archarius shrugged his shoulders and spat on the floor. "Our lands are at war, corruption breeds everywhere and the sick lay suffering and dying." Jesus replied, "As the heavens are higher than the earth so are my ways higher than your ways and my thoughts than your thoughts" (7). Jesus continued, "The Spirit of the Lord is on me, because he has anointed me to preach good news to the poor. He has sent me to proclaim freedom for the prisoners and recovery of sight for the blind, to release the oppressed, to proclaim the year of the Lord's favor" (8). Again, Archarius scoffed, "Promises of freedom and more, from a beaten man caged in a cell?"

Archarius asked, "How is your god any different than any of the others?" Jesus answered, "Acknowledge and take to heart this day that the Lord is God in heaven above and on the earth below. There is no other" (9).

"I will give you this, Jesus of Nazareth, your words do confuse me and they stay in my ears, but you priests often speak in riddles. If you actually thought to speak more plainly to the people, maybe you would add more followers to your fold." Archarius went on, "When I was young, I believed in justice, I believed in kindness and mercy; these things I had held dear and as I grew into a man, I saw them fall one by one as they were proven to be just the whims of women and poets. Your words remind me of those years, of those memories, but look around you, Jesus of Nazareth, what do you see? Tell me, truly, what do you see?" Jesus had closed his eyes and seemed to have stopped listening. Archarius waited for an answer, he waited for an argument from the man in the cell. Now growing angry and frustrated, Archarius barked, "Why do you not answer me? Perhaps because you have no defense? Why am I wasting my time speaking with such a mad man?" Archarius got up and started pacing back and forth in front of the cell. He turned suddenly and yelled at Jesus, "You speak of freedom, yet you're in a cell; you speak of good News, but there is none to be found, you speak of healing the sick, yet there you sit in a pool of your own blood. Do you really expect anyone to listen to you, to consider what you say, to actually become followers of this madness of which you preach? Do I wish your words were true? Do I wish we both were not here in this filthy hole? Do I wish I did not have to sleep every night with my sword close to my hand? Do I wish we all treated each other like men instead of animals? Of course I do; any sane man would, but just saying it does not make it happen. Can you not understand that? Your words change nothing! What do you expect me to do? What could even one man do?"

Archarius was angry. His bitterness was starting to show and this usually led to a few days' worth of sullenness. He started to walk away when he suddenly spun around and in a moment of rage, threw his cup at the bars of the man's cell. The cup clanged against the metal bars and then ricocheted down the corridor. The water which had been in the cup flew through the bars and into the cell, spraying water on Jesus; yet he continued to sit peacefully with his back to the wall and his eyes closed, seemingly oblivious to the whole tantrum.

Archarius stood outside the cell of Jesus and stared at him. He knew now this man or priest or king was not going to allow himself to get involved in an argument. He seemed at least smarter than Archarius in that way. Once again, Archarius sat down in the corner. This time, he closed his eyes and began to let his mind wander. He allowed his thoughts to lead where they may and slowly he gave in to the eventual relaxation that came with this exercise. He sat quietly and listened and became alert to all he heard and all he felt.

His mind raced and then became still. It was clear and then became confused. His heart ached, but it rejoiced. These moments always started the same; he felt burdened with guilt over his wasted talents as well as his sins of sloth. He knew he had skills and talents that others did not possess; yet he did nothing with them. He also knew deep down he acted lazy. He never really knew if it was his ego or his conscience telling him he should have been more than a soldier. He felt it deep in his mind that he was destined for greater things, destined to be a man who understood the bigger picture and who could lead others to do better with the world they inhabited. At the same time, his insecurities or was it his common sense that told him that he could not be that man and he was just a childish dreamer and he would always be one?

After he went through this painful but regular torment, his mind would drift onto other thoughts. He wondered about the future and what would become of him. What he would do? What experiences would he have and what successes or failures lie ahead for him? Toward the end of these rituals, he would wonder about where he would eventually fall. How would he die? Would he be alone or would he just be part of thousands that would lie dying on a battlefield? Or would he live to be old and finally die in some dusty room a useless old man whom no one would miss? Is it too late to change what was to come or is all the future set in stone and what will be will be? He opened his eyes, the anger gone but replaced with sadness. He wished instead he was still angry.

Chapter 14

Jesus opened His eyes and looked over at the poor creature sitting in the corner confused and frightened. He had pity for all those like Archarius, those who were searching but were too blind to see the truth. He breathed in deeply this stale foul air which proved so important to His body. For a moment, He allowed Himself to really experience the pain and brokenness of His body. He allowed Himself to feel the mortality and the moment by moment existence of this humanity. He experienced the fear that His children did and His eyes began to well with tears. Changing His thoughts to the Father, He again filled His mind with the strength of the Holy Spirit. Turning His attention now to Archarius, He continued to do the work for which He had come, to save His sheep, even if it meant one lamb at a time.

Remembering the words Archarius used in his anger and his pleas for simple instruction, Jesus called out to him. "Archarius, come speak with me." Archarius looked over to see Jesus smiling at him and beckoning him to come closer. His anger had subsided and he now felt quiet but somewhat disillusioned. For the moment, their roles of prisoner and guard were forgotten and Archarius stood up and walked over to Jesus.

'What do you wish to speak of?" he asked Jesus.

Jesus smiled again and sat down on His side of the cage and said, "You, Archarius, I want to know about you. Neither of us is apparently able to sleep, so let us talk and discuss any subject you like, but first I would like to learn more about you." Jesus silently chuckled as He already possessed all there was to know about Archarius, but it would be interesting to hear what events Archarius chose to divulge to Him.

Archarius walked over and stood in front of the bars of the cell. *This has been a most unusual night,* he thought to himself, *too many past memories, this very strange man and the peculiar curiosity he has stirred in me.* He looked toward the end of the corridor where there remained only darkness. *I will talk with this man,* he settled within himself, *anything to help pass away this wretched night.* "My name is," "Archarius, yes, I know," Jesus said softly, interrupting him. "Yes, well, you must have heard me called by name." Archarius continued, "I am a Roman Soldier," and then stopped, embarrassed the absurdity of his statement. "I mean, I like being a Roman soldier," and he stopped again. "I want..." and he hesitated. Jesus put up a hand as if to stop his tormented struggle with his conversation. "Tell me how you feel. what you see, what you want." Archarius wanted to say, *I feel fine, I see you locked in a cell and I want to go home,* but he chose not to be glib. Instead he replied, "I dislike guard duty immensely. I tire of seeing the worst of man and the filth and brutality. I want..." He hesitated again and then continued, "I want the world to be a just and enjoyable place like the world I imagined when I was just an innocent child." "Good," Jesus said softly, "Those are honorable thoughts, but what about you?" "Me?" Archarius answered, "What about me? I am a poor soldier who guards prisoners. I have no wife nor children and no real family nearby. My goal is to first, stay alive, second, not to be completely poverty stricken and third, to try to have a decent life until the merciful end. Those certainly don't seem like honorable thoughts, but they are necessary ones in this city."

Jesus slowly shook His head, "When so much is focused on the self and not your brothers, no, those are not statements of honor. You must take care of each other, don't you see? Focusing on just your own trials will not bring you the world you ask for; you must seek to care for each other."

"Let us start again," Jesus said. "Why do you not just leave this place?" "Leave and go where?" Archarius snapped back. "Where am I to go? I told you I have no family; my only friends are soldiers and they are not much better off than I am. No, I am stuck here, unbelievably talking with you. There is nowhere I can go; that is why I am still here." Jesus waited for a moment and asked, "So is it because you have no family and no friends outside of your fellow soldiers that have you in this desperate position?" Archarius paced back and forth, "Yes, are you not listening to me at all?" Jesus continued, "So without others who are in better position than yours, you have no options, you have no purpose.

How horrible and how unnecessary this is for you." Jesus looked directly at Archarius and said, "But what about your gods? Do they not help you or comfort you?" Archarius knew this was a baited question, but he answered it anyway. It had been a long time since he had so open a conversation and the discussion made him feel intelligent and more like an honorable citizen than a soldier. "I don't know which god you represent, but they have never showed any favor for me. There are so many people building altars and then dutifully paying homage. Why and to what end? There seems to be an endless amount of gods." Archarius did lower his voice as he understood his thoughts were indeed blasphemous thoughts. "These gods, how do I know they even exist? How do I know that the Senate didn't arrange all this to keep us all in line? Where are these gods when I see children dying in the alleys and women treated like dogs? Why should I build an altar to a god who doesn't even offer wisdom or rescue? Also, tell me, this priest if that is what you really are, which god is yours and to what aspect of our lives is he supposed to protect and why in Caesar's name doesn't he do anything about all this?" Archarius was angry now and he had never really had the chance to let off some of the anger on this subject to anyone for obvious reasons.

Jesus began speaking with a soft and kindly tone, "You must be of a calm mind and spirit to hear what I have to say about the one true God. Perhaps now is not the time" and Jesus started to turn away. "Perhaps now is not the time?" Archarius asked incredulously. "You are hours away from likely being executed. When do you think would be a good time?" Jesus replied, "If rain falls on hard soil, it just flows off of it and is wasted in the gutter, but if it falls on soft open soil, it seeps in and gives it life. Like the rain, so are My words; they must fall on open minds and open hearts so that their meanings may nurture and provide strength. I can help you for I am the Shepherd and you are the lost sheep. Hear My call and be comforted by it; let it lead you back to the flock where you will be safe and thrive."

Archarius drew a slow breath and walked over to the water barrel and helped himself to a drink. He turned and facing Jesus he said, "Your words confuse me, that is what they do for me. As for your role as a shepherd, how do I know you are not a man possessed and more like the wolf or the lion?" But Jesus' words had already had an effect on Archarius. Because as he would have done if another soldier had been with him and not a prisoner, he filled up the cup with water, walked over to Jesus and handed it to Him, all the time speaking his questions regarding the wolf and the lion. Jesus smiled and took the cup of water without saying a word about this action which in itself was extraordinary.

Accepting the cup back from Jesus, Archarius continued, "These words of yours that are proposed to be so much of a comfort to me, I am sure I have heard them before by others. Perhaps not as strange as you, but there are only so many words men can use before they just start repeating what had already been said." Feeling quite wise Archarius smiled and said, "See, I am not just a simple guard. I listen, I read and I learn." "It is not a dumb animal that you confer with," Jesus sighed and stole a look up toward his Father, saying to Himself,

Is this naïve soul your answer to My prayers, a simple diversion to help pass these difficult hours? You are indeed great, Father, and I am thankful for Your love and mercy.

Turning back to tender His sheep even though His own hours were numbered, Jesus stared at Archarius and decided He would enjoy saving this soul that His Father had provided to Him. "Archarius," Jesus called, "My words were created and formed in heaven and they are right now, right this very minute being offered to you. Hear them and learn not as a dumb animal but as a man made in the image of the Father. I will share this glory with you and I will answer your questions; you need only to be the plant which soaks up the warmth and nourishment of the "Son."

It was how Jesus looked as He said these words and how His voice sounded and how everything else seemed to have faded into the background that mesmerized Archarius so that he stood silently and then obediently sat down in front of the bars. Jesus nodded and He began to teach.

Chapter 15

"My words," said Jesus, "must be used and lived and not just heard; these are the words of life."

Jesus continued, truly sounding like a teacher, "I will show you what he is like who comes to me and hears my words and puts them into practice. He is like a man building a house who dug down deep and laid the foundation on rock. When a flood came, the torrent struck that house but could not shake it, because it was well built. But the one who hears My words and does not put them into practice is like a man who had built a house on the ground without a foundation. The moment the torrent struck that house, it collapsed and its destruction was complete" (10).

"Do you understand the meaning of this?" asked Jesus. "Yes, of course I do," answered Archarius. "Every man understands the difference between something well-constructed and one poorly constructed." "Yes," said Jesus, "but do you see how this will also apply to the type of man you are? If you are a man whose purpose is one of self service and thievery and corruption, his is a life of poor design and thought."

"Yes," said Archarius, "I agree; I understand what you are telling me." "Good," Jesus replied and He continued to make the point to Archarius: "A farmer went out to sow his seed. As he was scattering the seed, some fell along the path; it was trampled on, and the birds of the air ate it up. Some fell on rock and when it came up, the plants withered because they had no moisture. Other seed fell among thorns which grew up with it and choked the plants. Still other seed fell on good soil. It came up and yielded a crop, a hundred times more than was sown" (11).

"So you see," explained Jesus, "the man needs to be of good substance so that the words of life may grow and enrich the man himself. If the words of life are heard by one who only pretends to care, the words will not take root and the man will not be saved." "Saved from what?" Archarius asked. "Saved from a bad life, one of poverty or sickness?" "You must listen to all that I have to tell you before I explain the treasure that is offered to you," replied Jesus. "Tell me this then," Archarius asked. "I understand the good man and the good life he should live, but to whose laws? Who decides what is good?"

Jesus spoke, "All is supplied for you, and you need only to listen to My words and also to read the words given to you by the Father before I came to you. The Father provided specific laws of which man is to follow. Some of man's laws mirror the Father's but some do not. It is critical to your receipt of the great treasure that you follow My Father's commandments and not just the ones that man has mirrored with his laws. Man has made and continues to make many laws and man continues to worship many false gods. These false gods are houses of weak foundations and will not stand under duress. A man who follows every law of man but only some of My Father's laws will not receive the greatest treasure." Archarius stood and stretched his legs, speaking as he walked back and forth in front of the bars. "Yet, we must follow man's laws or else be put in prison." Jesus replied, "You may follow the earthly laws set down by man as long as they do not conflict with the spiritual laws of the Father. To do this successfully, you must know and understand all the laws of My Father, for the treasure He offers you is worth enough to spend your entire life in an earthly prison." "How am I to remember all that you say tonight? How am I to understand all these laws you speak of?" asked Archarius. Jesus replied, "The Father who is great and merciful has arranged to give you a key to the treasure, one that will reside inside of you and guide you. This will be made clearer to you in just a few days' time."

Archarius wanted to mention that in a few days it was likely Jesus may not be here to explain that statement, but he chose not to bring this up as he was strangely excited to be listening to the words of Jesus. Archarius sat back down and said, "Please, explain more of how a good man should live according to your laws."

"I will tell you of those who will be rewarded" and Jesus stood and looked up, closed His eyes and began to speak these words:

"Blessed are the poor in spirit, for theirs is the kingdom of heaven.

Blessed are those who mourn, for they will be comforted.

Blessed are the meek, for they will inherit the earth.

Blessed are those who hunger and thirst for righteousness, for they will be filled.

Blessed are the merciful, for they will be shown mercy.

Blessed are the pure in heart, for they will see God.

Blessed are the peacemakers, for they will be called sons of God.

Blessed are those who are persecuted because of righteousness, for theirs is the kingdom of heaven" (12). After Jesus had recited those words, He explained to Archarius that He needed to pray and again sat with His back against the wall and closed His eyes.

Chapter 16

Archarius, sitting back on the stool by the old water barrel, recognized that old sense of frustration coming back. Suddenly the headache began, the beginning of a fever, all the familiar symptoms brought on by his inability to comprehend the subject at hand. He despised this experience; it had plagued him for years and he recognized the onset and he knew the outcome and most of all, he knew the reason for it. It was his inability to bring his thought process to the next level. Was the issue his lack of intelligence or just a lack of focus or perhaps just an inability to process information he didn't know? What he did know was that the things he had just heard made little sense to him at all. Jesus had said blessings for the weak and also blessings for the poor and the merciful? What madness was he listening to? He felt his heart begin to harden and the sneer began to return to his face. His mind was tired of going back and forth between student and soldier, one moment, yearning and hoping for wisdom and in another, turning away and scowling at the attempt. His head was pounding now as he sat there debating within himself. His eyes were closed and he was rubbing his temples so hard that the hair felt like it was starting to loosen at the roots. He didn't want to open his eyes, he didn't want to see Jesus, he didn't want to hear Jesus, and he wanted this night to be over and this conflict in his head to be resolved. He seemed like two different people or just one man being pulled into two. Both sides were demanding him to choose and give way to that direction. His head was really hurting now and he sensed the old anger welling up inside of him. He had felt so peaceful just a few moments ago and now he thought he was close to insanity. He suddenly screamed out, "What do you want from me?"

Archarius opened his eyes, expecting to see Jesus standing where he had left Him, but He had returned to the corner of His cell and sat with His back against the wall, His eyes closed and His face was lifted slightly upward. Archarius was embarrassed, annoyed and physically ill; he wasn't sure what symptom held the majority, although he guessed his headache would be the victor. What had just happened to him? He, a Roman soldier, was about to sit like a school boy and listen to a prisoner in a cell! The next thing he knew, the pain in his head had begun and he felt the distrust and hatred rising to the surface. He must be going insane. He had heard about maladies that began with painful headaches and then led to madness or death. This must be what is happening to him, him at just 30 years old! He began to feel the panic a man experiences when the horror of insanity is now considered a possibility.

Archarius suddenly became very afraid. He sat on his stool, looking into the dark pool of the water barrel next to him, his mind racing with all the consequences of what insanity would mean. What would happen to him? He would be thrown out of the army, ostracized from the city, cast off to live on the outskirts of civilization, scraping out a pathetic existence. He felt his shoulders start to tremble as his confidence began to leave him. At that moment, Jesus, without opening His eyes or moving His head, said softly, "It is not madness that affects you; you are not the problem at all. It is the sin of man that pulls you away from Me."

The headache began to fade with the sound of Jesus' voice and Archarius opened his blood-shot eyes and stared at Jesus. "What do you mean by that?" he asked Jesus. Jesus slowly rose and replied, "While you are on this earth, the choice of how you live and which path you follow is yours. I will not push you down the path of righteousness; you must choose and find it on your own and even more importantly, you must remain on it in times of trial. He who is against Me will entice you to take the easier path, the path of selfishness and deceit. This evil one has always been here misleading and tormenting God's children. Now I am here to show you the way out of his grasp and onto the path that will lead you into the kingdom of Heaven. Alas, I cannot take you there with Me; you must complete the journey on your own, and he who is against Me will plan many pitfalls and hardships to confuse you and turn you against the Father. He is sin and he is evil and he is temptation. He will fool you with his lies, for he thinks only of himself. You must listen to what I tell you and remember all that we will discuss tonight, for as time goes by, the evil one will fade your memory and test your faith. I am the Good Shepherd and I am the Light that will remove darkness from the lives of My children. They need to only follow My word, love one another and worship the Lord thy God. Now, drink the water and refresh yourself. You will find it cool and pure, for very soon we must begin again."

Chapter 17

Archarius considered Jesus' comments regarding choosing the right path. Archarius had used the same analogy when he had thought about right and wrong. Once again his memory brought him back to the incident which continued to trouble him, the time fate thrust him into turmoil and he had definitely chosen the wrong path. Archarius had not actually chosen the wrong path; more accurately, he simply found himself set upon it. He never even remembered the process of choosing, everything had happened so fast and his immediate reaction had cursed his future. As the years had gone by, this event had become a terrible burden to him, one to be carried in his mind and in his heart for years. Archarius had just become a soldier and a very young one, as he was only 16. While some boys appeared as young men at 16, Archarius appeared more like a boy in men's clothing. His body had not yet filled out, the weight of muscle had yet to determine his outline and his face betrayed his youthfulness. Yet, he was of age and his father had been well known to those whom he had first contacted with his wish to join, so he was brought quickly into the fold.

His first two years consisted mostly of training and running errands as he waited for his body to catch up with his age and his desires of pursuing glory and adventure.

This was the young man who found himself walking alone on the outskirts of the city as he ran his last errand on that fateful afternoon.

Archarius enjoyed wearing the uniform of a Roman soldier. He felt great pride and the uniform gave him the confidence he was lacking, due to his size. He always traveled on his errands holding his spear more like a walking stick than the lethal weapon for which it had been designed. Due to his diminutive size, the spear made him appear more formidable than the sword. His sword was heavy and his forearms had not yet acquired the strength to wield it as he had been trained. The spear, however, would on this day prove to be far more burdensome to him. The afternoon was cooler than most and he hurried through the dusty streets made narrow by the stone sides of the rear facings of homes or workshops. The traffic in the streets typically thinned at this time of day as most people were now relaxing, their workday completed by midafternoon as they had begun work at dawn with the rest of Rome. The din that was Rome in the morning and early afternoon had subsided and things were actually almost peaceful. To Archarius, the streets were like a maze as buildings had been added, torn down and built again in different shapes and sizes. One could easily be lost or get lost, as many thieves relied on these interweaving streets for that very thing. His mind returned to the present and he shuddered as the memories came flowing back to him. He can still remember the moment all so clearly, just two quick moments in time tied together by only him and his actions.

On that particular afternoon Archarius had entered yet another street narrow like all the rest when he suddenly heard a frightening scream from someone nearby that he couldn't see. The sound had frightened him badly. A second later, on his left, the shape of a man burst out of the shadows, yelling and waving his arms. Archarius panicked and swung his spear wildly around from his right to his left while screaming at the same time. The head of the spear caught the shape and plunged deep into the neck and tore down to the hip before disengaging and continued its flight to the ground. Suddenly, all became quiet and Archarius with the spear now in his left hand stood frozen in place, unable to move as he watched the shape seemingly much smaller than he first thought slowly crumble to the ground. A moment later, he saw the blood starting to flow from under the cloak, mixing with the dirt to form dark black pools around the fallen shape. Faces appeared from the roof, doors opened and people suddenly began to appear in the street. Then an old woman came out of a doorway, stared down at the cloaked shape in the dirt and started screaming as she fell to her knees, clutching at the shape which lay in the dirt amid the blackening pools of blood and sand. She removed the cloak that covered the shape's face to expose the closed and lifeless eyes of a teenage boy. She screamed at Archarius, "You killed my son! Why have you killed my son?" The crowd started to grow and the narrow street was soon choked with strangers all staring at him and starting to grumble among themselves. This was the moment that the two paths presented themselves to Archarius. He chose quickly, "I did not kill your son," he stammered, "I found him lying here, just as you have, I did not kill him, I didn't." Why did he lie? He has wondered why for all these years. Was he afraid of what would have happened? Surely they would not have assaulted a Roman soldier. Did he think, then, that he would be charged with a crime? Of course not; people died every day in this city and this boy foolishly surprised an armed soldier and predictably it cost him his life. Why then? Archarius' mind was racing, stammering out falsehoods and fabrications about his arrival and his discovery of the body. He had buried the head of his spear in the dirt under the pretense of putting it aside so he could assist, but he knew there would be blood on the tip and the bloodied spear must not be discovered by this crowd of angry people. He was surprised and also concerned how easily the lying and the cover-up actually came to him. As the moments passed, his manner became calmer and he was more confident in his story. Who were these people to question his word? With a final stammer of condolence, he stated he would report the incident to his superior and hurriedly left the scene. He had no intention to and he never did report the incident.

For days, every time his name was called, he expected to see a unit of guards marching toward him to make an arrest and take him away to be thrown into prison. Finally, after two weeks, he began to relax. There were so many thousands of people living in this city and so much death unknown to most that he never even heard of the incident again and his identity was never known to the people back in that narrow street. In the following months, he avoided that area of the city and as the years went by, his looks matured and he no longer resembled the boy soldier. Only in his thoughts was the killing still being played out, sometimes brought on by something he would see, but mostly it appeared in his dreams. That dreadful afternoon would be a burden, a yoke around his neck, one that would follow him always, of that he knew for sure.

Chapter 18

A rcharius had always believed in evil, though he spent little, if any, time thinking about good. *Why, he thought, is evil so much easier to believe in than good? It had always seemed difficult to believe there is something good in the world looking out for us. Perhaps this seems true because there is such a strong evidence of evil in the world for us to see. The wars, the fear and the hatred were evident and everywhere; however, the evidence of good was easy for one to turn a blind eye.* He thought how wonderful it would be if he actually could believe there is someone or something which has his best interests at heart and is committed to guiding him and watching over him. What a wonderful world it would be if that were true. If this goodness did actually exist, Archarius decided, it certainly wasn't doing a very effective job. He turned and stared at the man called Jesus, Who sat beaten, bloody and imprisoned in a locked cell.

Archarius hoped Jesus wasn't the only one on the side of good, for it didn't appear to Archarius goodness was winning the battle. Archarius had always prided himself on having a logical mind. He considered he must give more thought to the side of good since he had already confirmed his belief of evil in the world. He decided the time had come to hear from the other side, assuming, of course, that this man in the cell wasn't just insane. He dipped the poorly formed and dented tin cup into the water barrel and slowly drank the water as he stared at Jesus. He stopped halfway through the drink and looked at the water barrel with a look of surprise on his face. This water which had been in this barrel for days and was usually tepid and flat was suddenly crisp, cool and perhaps the most refreshing water he had ever tasted. When he looked back toward the cell, Jesus was staring at him and said, "If the Father can make such a simple thing as water so refreshing how much more so can He make the soul refreshed? It is by studying the Word of the Father that one is renewed and put on the path to righteousness." Jesus continued, "As you have debated within yourself and just now decided to hear these words, let us begin again." Archarius was about to ask how Jesus knew what he had been thinking; however, he dismissed the thought as he saw Jesus standing, waiting as a teacher would wait for the class to settle down.

Jesus began: "My Father had made a covenant with His children many years ago. He did this by giving them simple laws to follow. However, those laws have been followed by few, ignored by many and unheard of by most. It is My Father's wish that I, His Son come to His children to live among them, speak with them directly and to provide parables that they might see the way. I have taught many but not nearly enough and before I finish my Father's work, I will teach you so that I may prepare a room for you in My Father's house." Archarius asked, "I don't understand why you wouldn't teach everyone if that is Your Father's wish." Jesus replied, "His wish is not that I teach all His children. I have planted the seed of glory within you as a people. The responsibility is yours to nurture and share the Word with each other, re-planting the seed again and again until the whole earth is covered in His Glory." "What if I just can't understand what you are trying to teach me?" asked Archarius, thinking back to his earlier frustration. Jesus replied, "All are able to understand, for the very rocks themselves could comprehend the laws if the Father wished it so. Worry not about your mind, for it is your heart through which the Holy Spirit will enter you and bless you. Listen with your heart, the heart which has told you to take pity on the poor man whom you walk past each morning and to whom you choose to give a piece of fruit. The heart which makes you consider the beauty of the trees that you love so much and the sky and the stars at night that you have stood in awe of so many times. I know these things because the Father knows these things for We are One. It is your heart which must guide you, your heart that you must now learn to trust. Your mind will be confused and often will hold you back because your mind sees only reality and what it is able to touch and taste and see. Your heart which you will soon refer to as your faith will overrule your mind and proceed down the road of righteousness when your brain says the road is foolish and dangerous. But your faith will enable you to achieve things your mind could never even comprehend. Your faith will become your newest sense and the most important part of your being. Faith will protect you from evil and all that man's words can do to you. Your faith, once rooted in the Word, will protect you for all of eternity. The path is not easy and for some, the path is very long and very difficult as each of you must find your own way. But worry not, for as your faith becomes stronger, your burdens will become lighter and your feet will soon glide upon the road to Heaven."

Chapter 19

Faith, thought Archarius, he had faith, he had faith the sun would rise in the morning and another day would begin. He had faith this hunger he felt in his stomach would be cured by a hearty breakfast and unfortunately, he had faith this man in the cell would endure a very long day tomorrow. "I already do have faith," he said to Jesus, "but not in the things you speak of." Jesus sighed and replied, "You are not ready for the discussion of faith, for you need to believe and then develop faith but your mind is determined to race ahead. Yet I will answer your questions as you ask them. You do not have faith the sun will rise tomorrow. You believe it because you have seen it do so morning after morning for as long as you can remember. If the sun did not rise tomorrow, would you have faith that it would the next day or would you allow yourself to be plunged into fear and doubt that it would ever rise again? You believe in something because you heard or you had learned of it. You will have true faith in something when your heart and your soul tells you it is so, even though your mind and what your eyes see tell you the opposite. The world does not stand against you and argue with your belief that the sun will rise tomorrow, so how strong does your faith need to be? Would it simply change, based on pressure and new information? That is not faith; it is a learned opinion."

Archarius reflected on this for a moment as this man's words, although odd, did appear to him to be honest and true. Suddenly, he felt a shiver down his back and he felt cold and very afraid as the realization of Jesus' knowledge of his thoughts occurred to him. How did Jesus know about his thoughts regarding his faith in the sunrise? He looked at Jesus, the fear and uneasiness displayed plainly on his face. Jesus turned to face him; Archarius was surprised as he thought he saw a quick wink as Jesus said, "You have nothing to fear; let your faith begin here, with me."

"Let us begin," Jesus continued, "all that you see and all that you touch has been given to you by the Father. You, as well as all men, have been created by the Father for His glory. You have been put upon this earth to serve Him." 'But how?" interrupted Archarius. "Why isn't He one of the gods we know? How do we serve something unknown to us?" Jesus answered sternly, "The gods you know are false. They have been made by man and are not of the Father. You pray to nothing; these gods live only in the minds of men. There is only one true God, God the Father." "But why is He unknown to us?" Archarius asked. Jesus answered, "He is not unknown to all His people. God spoke to man two thousand years ago when He spoke to His servant Moses and gave him the laws for all men to live by. But man chose not to listen and not to obey, so today many do not know of these laws. I have come from the Father to remind you of His laws and to teach you further truths. One of the greatest gifts given to man from the Father is the gift of life here on earth. Also is the gift of choice, to live as man sees fit, to listen, to see and to choose how to live. Man has been given the choice to live as one with the Father or to live apart, serving himself. These were the paths I spoke of to you: one path, the path of righteousness, leads to the Father and His house; the other, while temporarily pleasing, leads to eternal torment. Now that I have come, it is through Me that you will find your way to My Father's house. I bring a new covenant to man, one that will be revealed soon and one that will stand forever."

Archarius sighed, thinking for a moment and said, "I do not know of this Moses who lived so long ago. Who was he, a Roman? His name certainly doesn't sound like a Roman." Jesus smiled and said, "No, he was a Jew who lived far away from here. Moses was not the only man My Father had spoken with; there were more before him but indeed, none of them were Romans." Archarius shrugged and considered the Jews. They were an old and secretive people, they with their temple and their many laws. "Are the laws of the Jews the laws you speak of?" he asked. This time it seemed that it was Jesus' time to sigh. "The laws of My Father were given to His people in the hope that they would cast them like seed upon the people of the earth. Some have done so, but more have kept the seeds for themselves so that they might control the multitudes. My words are for all of God's children: the Jews, the Romans and people that you have not yet even learned exist. My words are for all the people who inhabit this earth and for those who are not even a dream in their mother's heart." Archarius again burst out full of questions, "Why does not Your Father just show himself and rule the earth? Why does He give laws to so few? Why does He send you to be abused and captured?" Jesus answered, "The Father created man for His glory. What glory would there be in a world enslaved to honor Him? The Father has given His children the greatest gift of all. He had bestowed upon them the intelligence that separates them from the animals and allowed them to possess a free will to choose their own path of life. It is His wish that all men choose to love and honor Him on their own in their own time and of their own free will. You cannot order a child to love its mother. You care for, you love and you teach the child in the hope that it recognizes the blessing of love and returns it to the parent. Man must learn to love their own kind before they can truly love God, for if they despise their fellow man, how can they love and honor Him who created his fellow man? Let no man who holds hatred of another man come before the Father unless he first makes amends with his brother.

One of the Father's greatest laws is that you love one another; if you cannot uphold that law, you cannot truly honor the Father. The words of the Father are like I have told you. They are the finest crop that man can possess and I am here to provide man with the seeds of that crop. They must be used by man properly, sowed with care, nurtured with the water of kindness and understanding and harvested with wisdom and love. When these seeds have covered the earth and blossomed, many rewards will be bestowed upon God's people. I come to man as a lamb to the lions; my way is pure and innocent. If I came as a lion, my words would be obeyed by fear instead of worshipped as the only truth. There are none who are afraid of Me, only those who feel as if they compete with me for my Father's flock. Those should indeed fear the wrath of the Father, for those who lead astray the children of the Father will suffer for all eternity." Archarius interrupted again, "Your Father will do harm to these people that upset His plans? You speak of lambs and loving all Your fellow man, but then You speak of retribution for some people. I thought You said Your Father prepares a room for everyone." "Yes," Jesus replied. "My Father does indeed prepare a room for all of His children within His kingdom. It is the hope that all will hear the truth and choose to accept it, for nothing would please My Father more than to have all His children in His house. My Father is a just God and will reward all His people who follow His laws and the examples I have left for you. The precious gift of life and free will is not without danger. Those who know the truth of My Fathers words and turn away and bring evil against their fellow man will be sent away from His kingdom to a place too terrible to show you. It was their choice to refuse the gift they were given, to turn away from love and glory and choose selfish pleasures. These will never see the room reserved for them by the Father." Archarius considered these words and the seriousness of Jesus' tone. He did not know if it was from fear of the previous topic or his yearning for more of his teaching, but he suddenly asked, "Tell me these laws your Father gave the man called Moses." Jesus nodded and started to recite the laws:

* "I am the Lord your God; you shall have no other Gods before me.

* Thou shall not make any graven image of anything in the heavens, in the earth below, or in the waters under the earth. Thou shall not bow down to them or adore them for I am the Lord thy God.

* Thou shall not take the name of the Lord thy God in vain.

* Remember to keep Holy the Sabbath day.

* Honor thy mother and thy father.

* Thou shall not kill.

* Thou shall not commit adultery.

* Thou shall not steal.

* Thou shall not bear false witness against thy neighbor.

* Thou shall not covert thy neighbor's wife."

As Jesus finished speaking, He closed His eyes and appeared to be praying. Archarius thought to himself, *heaven is going to be a pretty lonely place if all those rules are enforced*. There wasn't anyone he knew, including himself, that wasn't guilty of breaking at least half of the laws Jesus had just listed for him. He started to walk away, shaking his head when he heard Jesus speak, "God knows the hearts of man and knows that man is a sinner. The Father has brought Me for more than one purpose. Man has both the sin he was born with and the sins he himself commits. God has designed ways for man to be absolved of both." Archarius turned around and said with a slight tone of frustration, "What do you mean, born with? How can we be born sinful?" Jesus replied, "You are not born sinful; you are born human and man is a fallen soul. He carries the sin of the first man with him as part of his punishment. Listen to me and know the Grace of God. All sins that have been and will be are to be forgiven by the Father, once My work here is done. The Grace of God is equal to His glory." Rubbing his temples and leaning up against the bars of the cell, Archarius said slowly, "If your work, whatever that may be, is to erase these old sins as well as the new sins, then are not the laws you listed unnecessary as those sins will be forgiven, too? If all of us are to be forgiven for everything we do, who are these people that are going to be turned away from your Father's house? None of this is making any sense to me and I'm still trying to figure out why I am even standing here debating this with you." "You have listened and heard many things," Jesus said to Archarius. "Go, sit and drink some of the cool water that so refreshed you just a little while ago. You will find it will now refresh more than just your thirst."

Chapter 20

Archarius sat on the wooden stool in the corner of the dark and dank hallway stretching along the row of cells; all were empty but one. He breathed heavily and sipped the cool delicious water out of the dented and mangled metal cup. He looked at this man called Jesus, this man who may be responsible for the most peculiar night in his life. *Jesus was right about one thing,* he thought, *I am beginning to feel better.* He could feel the cool water going down his throat into his stomach and cooling his frustration as well as his thirst. He had always enjoyed the moment when he closed his eyes and simply enjoyed a drink of cold water. It had always calmed him down. He compared the experience to taking that big breath before trying something for the second time, something you failed at previously, a simple breath and a drink of water and a man became rejuvenated and stood ready to try the impossible again. *We are simple creatures,* Archarius thought, *not much above the animals in that manner, we only need the basics to keep on going.*

Archarius had always prided himself on acknowledging and appreciating the moment, something so few people he thought took the time to do. For example, yesterday he had been worrying about which duty assignment he would be scheduled to do next month, another term of guard duty or would he be sent out as a messenger or perhaps part of a scouting mission? Either way, these were not exactly life or death decisions. Now just one day later, he is talking through the bars to a man who proclaims Himself the one who is here to gain the forgiveness of not only Archarius' sin but those of the whole world. Even more unsettling was the struggle that he felt in his head: one dismissing him as a lunatic and the other more troubling and even frightening consideration, that He may speak the truth.

This possibility caused him to shiver deep inside. The unsettledness was the most curious sensation he had ever had, and it had a very troubling effect. Yes, the points Jesus made rang true, but they were so foreign in their nature. The basic aspects he understood, such as love is better than hate, peace better than war but these things can be accomplished just by man trying to do the right thing and they don't require the laws and influence of a god. What about all this forgiveness of sin? What is sin but something that someone else deems wrong? Isn't sin relative to the person who is judging the sin? Should what I consider a specific sin to be applied to all men? It certainly doesn't seem fair. What if others declared carrying a weapon to be a sin? Would I not be wise to carry a sword on the outskirts of the city? If the person who thought weapons were sinful lived his life here in the safety of a city made safe by those who had weapons, what logic is there is that? It has been many years since Archarius had put this much thought into anything that was outside his day to day life. There was always a side of him which knew there had to be much more than just being born, scratching out an existence and finally dying, but there were few he felt comfortable discussing this with. He often wondered why more people, no, why didn't everyone think this way? Are we all so simpleminded and so involved in our narrow-minded day to day issues that we cannot consider anything outside of our understanding? If all men somewhere deep down did not feel there was some ultimate consequence, why wouldn't the majority be murderers and thieves? No, we all know there is something; the argument may be what kind of something, not if there is something. With the exception of those who are just lying to themselves, Archarius believed all men believed in something at the end of life, but what exactly is where their agreements ended.

"It is a beginning to know that you do believe in something." These were the words he heard stinging him out of his daydream. He ran his hands through his hair while turning to look at Jesus who stood there saying nothing. "What did you just say?" he asked Jesus. Jesus acted as though He didn't hear him and continued, "Remember though, believing in the wrong thing is worse than not believing in anything at all. Be careful whom you follow for there is only one path to the Father. You have many questions, I know, and your questions will help you understand. However, what is important is that you recognize the word when you hear it so that your questions will be answered in truth. You have asked about sin and I shall tell you. The Father abhors sin, yet He is faced with this every day for man is a constant sinner. Sin with man is past, present and future. Until the Father ends this world as you understand it and brings home His flock, man will continue to sin. Man has been a fallen being since the time of his ancestor who committed the first sin. Since that moment, man has been a sinner. He so often chooses out of selfishness when given an opportunity, yet there is hope, for the Father has sent His only Son to erase the sin of the past, to teach you to recognize the sins of the present and to assure you that you will be forgiven the sins of the future. You ask why future sin will be forgiven and to what end. You ask why man would stop sinning if he knows of the grace of forgiveness. I tell you this: the Father knows the heart of man and by that knowledge, He will choose to forgive or condemn. If a man continues to sin because he thinks his slate will be wiped clean, then he is a fool and he will be condemned in judgment. If, however, a man sins, regrets his actions, truly repents and strives to commit that sin no more, he will be forgiven by the Father. There is no hiding the true face of man from the Father, for He sees you better than you see yourself. Man wants and needs to believe in something; sadly, this trait of man is the weakness the evil preys on, man's own needs. As a child needs its parent, man needs the Father. Like a child needs to be taught the difference between right and wrong, so does man need to be taught the Holy Word. Without the Word to teach him, man would become like the spoiled child: selfish, destructive and eventually evil. You, Archarius, are blessed for the Word has come to you. Will you open your heart and receive this blessing?" Jesus held up His hand as Archarius began to answer, "Speak not, My son, for your words are worthless; your actions and your life from this moment on will decide your fate." Jesus turned away and sat again with His back to the wall, His eyes closed and His face turned upward.

Chapter 21

Archarius had been nine years old when he first tasted the difference between good and evil. The bitter taste left with him had spurred him on to become a Roman soldier for he craved the control and discipline of the army. Archarius did like people when he dealt with them one on one, they mostly didn't frighten him at all. In fact, some were kind and pleasant to know; however, when they were in groups, they changed and became something else, something he didn't like at all. His father had told him that people draw strength and security from being part of a crowd. They became louder, more aggressive and less like themselves and more like the loudest person in the group. It was this change that he both feared and despised and this also nurtured his distrust of people in general.

While running errands for his mother after the midday dinner, Archarius would often stop at the Ferrarius shop to see the old toolmaker, Batto. Archarius knew almost all of the shop owners in the neighborhood and they would all call out hello to him as he walked by, but he liked Batto the best. He enjoyed watching him forge the iron sickles for the men who would cut down the harvest. Batto took great pride in crafting his sickles. They had long wooden handles, with his own carefully designed iron blade on the end. Archarius' father had told him Batto made some of the finest sickles in Rome. Archarius would lean against one of the wooden posts in Batto's shop and ask him question after question about almost anything. Batto seemed to enjoy his company and rarely seemed frustrated by the incessant questions fired at him from Archarius. Batto would answer as best as he could often with a story to back up his opinion. When he didn't know the answer or perhaps didn't want to admit not knowing the answer, he would just shrug and mutter, "That subject is best left for you to figure out. I have given you too many answers already today." Archarius visited Batto's shop as often as he could, for he loved the stories and believed he learned more from this old iron-worker than he did from his studies. When on his way to the shop, he would often bring a large pear from home, for this was a favorite of the old toolmaker and it would entice him to stop work for a moment to eat while young Archarius riddled him with this day's batch of questions. From this keen eyed and plainspoken old man, Archarius obtained a new respect and interest in the history of the land and its resources. Here is where Archarius developed his imagination as he listened to the stories Batto told of his early days traveling the empire.

It was late afternoon one day as Archarius trooped down the road toward Batto's shop with yet another fine pear for his friend.

He heard the yelling of the crowd before he even reached Batto's shop. The crowd was two or three people deep in front of the shop. They were yelling at Batto and for what Archarius could gather, the crowd was blaming him for higher taxes they could not afford to pay. That didn't make any sense as Archarius knew the tax collector collected the taxes from the shop owners and he was the object of their scorn. Archarius stopped at the edge of the crowd and listened to the ranting as the angry men seemed to take turns hurling insults and accusations at Batto who Archarius still could not see because of the crowd. What mostly shocked Archarius was he recognized many in the crowd as the other shop owners, many of whom operated on this very street. He had always thought they were Batto's friends as they often passed by and stopped to say hello or to complain about business or taxes. As he listened to the ranting of the crowd, he began to piece together the problem.

Apparently, the tax collector had made a proposal to the merchants on the two closest streets that they should pay a small additional tax that would not be recorded and be given directly to the tax collector himself, obviously a payoff of some kind. Batto had refused to pay this corrupt fee, so the tax collector raised all their taxes even higher in retribution. The tax collector had even gone as far as to tell the suppliers to raise their prices of the bulk materials the shop owners bought for their individual trades. When they learned these penalties had been due to Batto's stubbornness, they turned on him in anger. An hour had gone by before Archarius actually caught a glimpse of Batto who looked very upset and harried. Suddenly, the crowd surged and took hold of Batto and carried him off. Archarius tried to follow, but some of the men were stopping anyone from following them. Archarius never saw his friend again and the next day, the shop was looted and left empty. Soon another merchant opened up a shop in Batto's location and it was like Batto never even existed. Archarius had no doubt the mob had taken his friend away and killed him but when he told his mother of this event, she believed they simply drove him out of the city. Yet, Archarius knew his friend was gone, he just felt it. He was frightened at how quickly men who acted as one's friends soon became their executioners. He didn't know if the other shop keepers were evil or if evil had just invaded their hearts for a time. Either way, Archarius saw a sample of the evil that seems to be just waiting to surface in men, if given just a small opportunity.

Chapter 22

"A re some men evil from the beginning?" Archarius suddenly asked Jesus. Jesus' eyes seemed to sadden at this question. "Yes, for the evil one takes even children from My Father's flock. He inhabits and corrupts their souls so they seek only self-serving means. It is one of this world's greatest tragedies that the young and innocent are abused in this manner." "Why does your Father permit it? Is He not more powerful than this evil one of which you speak?" Jesus spoke as He looked at His hands and rubbed the dried blood from His skin, "When man disobeyed the Father, he was cursed with his own destiny instead of the one the Father had chosen for him. In his simple mind, man desired this choice and this control, the ability to make decisions and choose his own path regardless of the laws of God. It was this decision that unleashed the enemy. It was this moment that provided an opportunity for an otherwise frustrated being which craved his own kingdom but possessed no avenue in which to create it. When man turned away from God, he became an unknowing victim for centuries to come, prey for the enemy. The

Father chose not to take away what He had given, so the freedom He blessed man with was also his sentence of death when he failed to use it wisely. So throughout time, the enemy has reigned and created terror and sadness for God's children in the manner of war, disease and disaster."

"Are you saying this is to go on forever like this?" asked Archarius. "No, my son," Jesus replied, "for God has sent His one and only Son to erase all sin and show man the path to His Father's house. It is by believing in Me, believing I am the Son of God and the following of My Father's laws which will lead man out of the grip of the beast and into everlasting joy in the house of the Lord." "But they mock you, beat you and they likely will kill you soon enough. What then? How will your Father feel when He sees we beat and murdered His Son? Will we not then have two enemies, this enemy you speak of and also a vengeful father?"

"No, for My Father knew of this result before He sent me. He knew of man's reaction; He even knew of our very conversation."

"This will be hard for you to listen to, Archarius my friend, but listen with faith and not with logic. The Lord our God is not a man so you cannot apply your logic to Him. It would be like expecting an ant to understand the source of the wind for you to try to rationalize His thoughts and actions. God is greater than anything your mind could even imagine or dream of and then a thousand times more. His ways are not your ways and His thoughts are not your thoughts. To try to compare them is fruitless. He is a thousand times more than the difference between you and the insect in the air. Man can mold mud into bricks, but God can turn dirt into life and then create a will and also intelligence. He can create love and joy, compassion and sacrifice. He can create all things or He can choose to create nothing."

Speaking almost as a child, Archarius asked, "I guess we are fortunate that He is a good God then, aren't we?" Jesus smiled and said, "Yes, My son, man is very blessed to have a Father who chooses to love him more than any other desire." "What about you?" Archarius asked. "Why should you be treated like this? Do we not need you here to teach us? Aren't you afraid you will be beaten more and likely killed?" "Yes," Jesus said slowly, "I am afraid, for I am part man and that part is very afraid, but My Father has sent His Holy Spirit to guard Me against doubt and to help Me to endure the sacrifice. I will do My Father's bidding, but I could not without His help. I have spent many years teaching, so like seeds spread upon the fields, they will take root and grow and with each harvest, they will become more numerous and of more heartiness until the Father calls   all his children home to His kingdom. This is the way to escape the evil one, for he knows My Father's plan but not the timing. so he will commit himself to spoiling as many seeds and harvests as he can to reduce the number of those who will go to my Father's house in the hope that they will, instead, serve him in hell.

You, My dear friend, must have faith in My teachings; you must ask for forgiveness of your sins and repent so that you may follow My teachings always. You must pray to the glory of

God. If you do these things, you will one day occupy the room My Father has made for you in His House."

Archarius approached the bars and softly spoke to Jesus, "I agree with your teachings, as they make sense to my heart. I'm not sure if that is what you mean by faith. However, I am troubled. I do not know how to pray, but I will try if you will show me how." Jesus answered, "Truth is indeed often heard first in the heart and then in the mind. Faith is a deeper resolve of which you will one day possess, but like a seed, a sprout comes before a stalk. To pray to the Father is both a privilege and a pleasure. God has referred to man as His children purposely, so the relationship would be one that you could understand. So as a child can be thankful for his father, so may you be thankful for your God. Be thankful for His love and attention; be thankful for His love and His mercy. Give thanks and glory to the Lord your God. A child asks things of his father and ultimately know that the father will do what he thinks is best for the child. So it is with man and his God. Ask for help in your troubles and your life and in His time and in His way, He will answer you. Be persistent in your prayers so that the Father knows your heart. Finally, as a child affectionately hugs his father, love your God with all your heart. Offer everything you do to His glory, follow His teachings and spread His word. This, dear Archarius, is how you should pray."

With that, the battered, bloody and beaten man dressed in rags sat back down against the wall of His cell. As He sat there and before He closed His eyes, He turned to Archarius and told him, "Pray now, My son, for I must do the same, for the hour of My destiny is approaching. We will talk one more time before that hour arrives." With that, Jesus closed His eyes and with His face pointed upwards, began to pray.

Chapter 23

As Jesus prayed, Archarius went back to the stool in the corner by the water barrel. As he sat on the small hard stool in the corner of this dark and miserable place, he considered all that he had heard this night. He had listened to many things that were both foreign and also fascinating. Most importantly, he heard words that stirred thoughts and feelings that had been buried deep inside him since his childhood. *What time is it*, he thought to himself, *the dawn can't be far away.* He was so very tired, more mentally exhausted than physically; as he considered the events of the past few hours, he closed his eyes and slowly slipped off to sleep.

Jesus opened His eyes and looked at Archarius as he slept. He whispered a prayer, smiled and closed His eyes again and returned to prayer.

In his dream, Archarius floated over the land, an unseen and unheard observer of the events below.

Down below him, he noticed a woman sitting on a donkey while a man, seemingly her husband, frantically searched from door to door pleading for a place to stay the night. Archarius could see the anxiety in the man's face as he tried unsuccessfully to find shelter. As the woman patiently sat waiting, the husband reluctantly settled for an offer to use a crude stable as shelter for the night. The situation was proved to be more serious as Archarius noted the woman was close to giving birth. Suddenly, Archarius was over the desert and witnessed a line of travelers down below walking in a straight line and seemingly looking up at him occasionally as if to get their bearings. Then he appeared behind them, looking up into the night sky, seeing what they saw: a large magnificent light shining so close it seemed he could touch it. He followed along behind this group of travelers as they seemed to search out the path to the star. As he followed, he saw the group approach the city and then finally, to his amazement, the very crude stable where the couple expecting the baby had been forced to sleep the night. The star seemed to hang over this very place, the light shining down like an energy filling the stable with light and warmth. Some of the men from the group knelt at the entrance to the stable and bowed their heads as if they were unworthy to enter this crude shelter.

Slowly, Archarius was able to see into the stable and he noticed that the woman had given birth and the baby was the focus of the travelers and their homage. The light from the star that had guided the group to this site seemed to shine directly on this baby and yet it also seemed like the light radiated from the boy himself. Archarius listened as the people started to gather at this stable, shepherds from the fields, the travelers and others whom he did not know. He listened as the shepherds told the small crowd that an angel had come to them while they were still in the field and said to them, "I bring you good news of great joy that will be for all the people. Today in the town of David, a Savior has been born to you; He is Christ the Lord. This will be a sign to you: you will find a baby wrapped in cloths and lying in a manger" (13). As Archarius heard these words, the knowledge came to him that he was witnessing the birth of his friend, the man in the cell.

All suddenly became bright and Archarius felt himself moving away to another destination. As the light abated and his eyes began to focus, he found himself floating over a river where people stood on the shores but for one very strange man who stood in the river shouting at the people on the shore, not in anger but in zeal. This was the man called John that he had seen that day when he had been travelling with his father years ago. He saw one person after another slowly walk out to this man who stood up to his waist in the river. The two in the water would speak first to each other and then as if to address the crowd. Following this, one would be put under the water and then they would both exclaim out loudly. Suddenly, he saw a man on the shore who looked familiar to Archarius. The man called John who stood in the river seemed to be afraid or nervous because of this man. As the two men spoke to each other, Archarius saw the man on the shore more clearly and realized He was the man in the cell! The man in the river immersed Jesus into the water and when He came out, Archarius saw the sky flash as the clouds parted and a bright light emitted a dove and Archarius heard the words, "This is my Son, whom I love, with Him I am well pleased"(14). As Jesus left the river, all this faded and again Archarius was blinded and began traveling to another destination.

When the mist cleared from his eyes, Archarius knew he had arrived at his next vision. He found himself inside a small house crowded with people, the air was dusty and the heat stifling. There seated inside were many people all crowded into the main room, awaiting something or someone. Soon, many Pharisees entered and sat among the people. Soon after, Jesus entered, looking strong and serene as He gazed at the crowd and made His way to the center of the room. How different Jesus looked from the man in the cell. He exhibited strength and confidence, but did so with just His posture and His gaze. There Jesus sat and He began speaking to the people.

The men called the Pharisees, who were many throughout the area, served as the teachers and translators of the scriptures for the people. They seemed to sneer and disapprove of Jesus speaking with so much authority. Jesus also began to heal the sick who begged His mercy. Suddenly, light came in from the roof as men had removed sections of the roof and began lowering a very sick man down on ropes so Jesus could heal him as the entrance to the house was too over-crowded with people trying to listen or gain entry. The man was paralyzed and appeared quite weak as he lay upon the lowered cot in front of Jesus. Jesus looked up at this poor man's friends who had gone to such extremes to place their stricken friend in front of Him. He said to them, "Friends, your sins are forgiven." This angered the Pharisees and Archarius could hear them speak under their breath, "Who is this man who speaks blasphemy and says he can forgive sins where it is law that only God has the power to forgive sins?" Jesus turned to them as if He had heard them but in the din of the crowd, that would have been impossible, and said, "Why are you thinking these things in your hearts? Which is easier to say, your sins are forgiven or to say get up and walk? But so you may know the Son of Man has authority on earth to forgive sins," He turned to the poor paralyzed man lying on the cot and said, "I tell you, get up, take your mat and go home." The man immediately stood up and praising God, picked up his mat and walked from the house. The people in the house were filled with awe and cried out to Jesus, but the Pharisees looked confused and startled by this event.

Archarius stood and vainly tried to make his way through the crowd toward Jesus, calling out His name but the clamor was too loud and the crowd too great in the small room and he became pushed farther back and then Jesus was gone. He tried to follow, but his eyelids grew heavy once again and the mist slowly began to fill his vision.

Archarius opened his eyes; his head was pounding and he felt dizzy. He found himself sitting under an olive tree at the foot of a hill. It was a calm but very warm day and the tree's branches shielded him from the hot sun. He rubbed his eyes and ran his fingers through his hair as he tried to grasp what was happening to him. One strange dream or vision after another and now another strange place. Was he awake or still dreaming? As he struggled with this thought, he noticed people in the near distance walking together off the road and toward the hills. He sat watching them as more and more arrived and began to gather toward the top of the nearest hill, but also they gathered along the sides of the hill. This vision seemed different than the others, for this time he felt as if he were alive and part of the time. He sat on the ground, not floating above and he was uncomfortable and aware of his body where before he focused only on what he saw and heard.

Archarius called out to a woman walking by, accompanying an old lady who was severely bent over and barely able to see where she was going. He called out again, but the woman had not heard him. That much seemed to be the same from the other vision in that he was unseen and unheard. He wondered why he was here and what he would witness. He soon grew restless and hungry and decided to follow the crowd as they walked toward the hill. He followed the woman and the old lady for a mile, but then lost them in the crowd as he approached the hill full of what must have been several thousand people. It was located in a desolate area with few trees and no homes or fields. The crowd had ceased moving and was now settled down in groups. He then heard a voice that seemed as if it were right next to him, but he soon ascertained it came from a man high up on the hill. The crowd became quiet and he heard a man nearby scold his children to be quiet as the rabbi Jesus was beginning to speak. *Jesus,* he said to himself as he now recognized the voice that mysteriously could be heard, even by the hard of hearing seated far away. Jesus spoke to the crowds as he had to Archarius from the cell.

He spoke of the kingdom of God and the house His Father prepared in heaven for all those who believed in Him.

When it had become late, the crowd grew restless as they knew they had far to travel to find any form of a dinner. In a flash, Archarius was again floating above the crowd and looking directly down upon Jesus and His assistants, he could hear them telling Jesus to dismiss the crowd, for most had far to go to find dinner. Jesus looked over at the meager supply of food brought by His followers meant for their own supper. He looked at His followers and said, "You will give the people food to eat." The followers were incredulous as they replied that they had only enough food for less than a dozen men and there must be five thousand people stretched out for a mile. Jesus, paying no attention to their objections, directed the people to gather in large groups. He took the five loaves of bread and the two fish the followers had brought and blessed them and looked up to heaven as He did so. He then broke off a piece of a loaf of bread and a portion of the fish and had it brought to one of the large groups of people. No matter how many people broke off pieces of fish or bread, the portion sent by Jesus did not end. Jesus did this with all the groups until all the people were fed. At the end, there were, incredibly, twelve baskets of bread left over that had not been eaten. Another flash of light shown in Archarius' eyes and he was again seated under the olive tree, now watching the people slowly make their way home. He saw the same woman, but this time she was with an elderly woman who stood straight and he heard her praising the Lord as she walked by and he realized that like the man in the house, she too had not only been fed but healed as well. With that realization, the mist visited Archarius again and his stomach tightened as he wished no more visions.

Chapter 24

Archarius awoke with a start as he looked at the dark corridor and the filthy cells and realized his visions were over. He was very thirsty and his head ached terribly. He looked over at Jesus who was watching him as he tried to make sense of his now familiar surroundings. "You need refreshment," Jesus told him. "Drink the water and let it cool your body and heal the pain in your head." Archarius dunked the battered metal cup into the water barrel and drank heavily for the water again tasted oddly very cold and very good. He slumped back against the wall on his stool as he finished the drink. Jesus broke the silence when He said, "You have been far and seen many things, dear Archarius, but your visions are not over." Archarius wanted to reply, but his tongue grew heavy and his eyes were closing and he knew he was again on his way.

When Archarius opened his eyes, he found himself in a small room with approximately a dozen men or so. It was quiet and the air was very still. The men were speaking to each other, but in low voices and they seemed very nervous.

The door opened with a burst of wonderfully refreshing cool air and Jesus entered the room. He walked to the center of the room and looking at each of the men, He seemed to feel their concerns, then He spoke, "Therefore I tell you, do not worry about your life, what you will eat or about your body and what you will wear. Is not life more important than food and the body more than clothes? Look at the birds of the air; they do not sow or reap or store away in barns, yet your heavenly Father feeds them. Are you not much more valuable than they? Who of you by worrying can add a single hour to his life? And why do you worry about clothes? See how the lilies of the field grow. They do not labor or spin. Yet I tell you even Solomon in all his splendor was not dressed like one of these. If that is how God clothes the grass of the field, which is here today and tomorrow is thrown into the fire, will He not much more clothe you, O you of little faith? So do not worry, saying, 'What shall we eat?' or 'What shall we drink?' or 'What shall we wear?' For the pagans runs after all these things, and your heavenly Father knows that you need them. But seek first His kingdom and His righteousness and all these things will be given to you as well. Therefore do not worry about tomorrow, for tomorrow will worry about itself. Each day has enough trouble of its own" (15). "Do not be afraid, little flock, for your Father has been pleased to give you the kingdom. Sell your possessions and give to the poor. Rather, provide purses for yourselves that will not wear out, a treasure in heaven, that will not be exhausted, where no thief comes near and no moth destroys.

For where your treasure is, there your heart will be also" (16).

Archarius heard these words and thought they were directed at him as his life has always been one of worry or dread. He worried almost every day about if he was smart enough or strong enough or respected enough or wealthy enough.

If one aspect seemed fairly secure, there were many others fears to take its place. What if this happens, what if that happens, what would he do then? He had always planned how he would react in the event of this crisis or that crisis; he seldom was at peace for he remained constantly fearful of tomorrow. These were very wise words of Jesus, but how does one accomplish that feeling, the trust that everything will be all right? As he looked around the room, watching the other men as they tried to assimilate what Jesus said to them, he remembered that one phrase Jesus had used, "O ye of little faith." Is that the key to the peace--faith? But faith is not something Archarius really understood. He understood the abstract of courage and he knew what courage meant and how one man could have it but not another. He also knew that someone who did not have courage could one day achieve it. But faith? Do I slay a lion to get faith as I would to obtain courage? What do I do to gain this faith?

Chapter 25

Archarius opened his eyes and he was again in the presence of Jesus and the group of men he had just seen with him. This time, however, they were outside in a small grove and Jesus was speaking: "Two men went up to the temple to pray, one a Pharisee and the other a tax collector. The Pharisee stood up and prayed about himself: 'God, I thank you that I am not like other men, robbers, evildoers and adulterers or even like this tax collector. I fast twice a week and give a tenth of all I get.' But the tax collector stood at a distance. He would not even look up to heaven but beat his breast and said, 'God, have mercy on me, a sinner.' I tell you that this man rather than the other went home justified before God. For everyone who exalts himself will be humbled and he who humbles himself will be exalted" (17).

This caused many in the crowd to be bewildered. People were also bringing babies and small children to Jesus so that He would touch them. As the men who were with Jesus saw this, they started to turn them away when Jesus stopped them. He said to the men, "Let the little children come to me and do not hinder them, for the kingdom of God belongs to such as these. I tell you the truth; anyone who will not receive the kingdom of God like a little child will never enter it" (18).

Later, when it was just Jesus and His followers, He said seriously to them, "The time is coming when you will long to see one of the days of the Son of man, but you will not see it. Men will tell you, 'There he is, there he is,' but do not go running after them. For the Son of man in His day will be like the lightning which flashes and lights up the sky from one end to the other. But first, He must suffer many things and be rejected by this generation. Just as it was in the days of Noah, so will it be in the days of the Son of man. People were eating, drinking, marrying and being given in marriage up to the day Noah entered the ark. Then the flood came and destroyed them all. It was the same in the days of Lot. People were eating and drinking, buying and selling, planting and building. But the day Lot left Sodom, fire and sulfur rained down from heaven and destroyed them all. It will be just like this on the day the Son of man is revealed. On that day, no one who is on the roof of his house with his goods inside should go down to get them. Likewise, no one in the field should go back for anything. Remember Lot's wife! Whoever tries to keep his life shall lose it and whoever loses his life shall preserve it. I tell you, on that night, two people will be in one bed, one will be taken and the other left. Two women will be grinding grain together, one will be taken and one will be left" (19).

Jesus' followers seemed greatly anguished with this and began whispering to each other as the mist came and swept Archarius away.

He knew he was leaving this vision and began to hope that he would wake up on his stool in the corner of the filthy hallway back in a life he understood. The mist cleared and he now stood in the middle of a crowd. It was hot and dusty and the people were all arguing among themselves. Archarius looked to the front of the crowd and saw Jesus speaking. He drew nearer and heard these words: "I tell you the truth, I am the gate for the sheep. All who came before Me were thieves and robbers, but the sheep did not listen to them. I am the gate; whoever enters through Me will be saved. He will come in and go out and find pasture. The thief comes only to steal and kill and destroy; I have come that they may have life, and have it to the fullest. I am the good Shepherd. The good shepherd lays down his life for his sheep. The hired hand is not the shepherd who owns the sheep. So when he sees the wolf coming, he abandons the sheep and runs away. Then the wolf attacks the flock and scatters it. The man runs away because he is a hired hand and cares nothing for the sheep. I am the good Shepherd; I know my sheep and my sheep know me--just as the Father knows me and I know the Father--and I lay down my life for the sheep. I have other sheep that are not from this sheep pen. I must bring them also. They too shall listen to my voice and there shall be one flock and one shepherd. The reason that the Father loves me is that I lay down my life, only to take it up again. No one takes it from me, but I lay it down of my own accord. I have authority to lay it down and authority to take it up again. This command I received from my Father" (20). The people in the crowd began arguing, some calling Jesus mad or a demon, but others were retelling the stories of the miracles Jesus had performed on the sick. Archarius tried to listen to both sides, but his head began to hurt until his eyes again focused on Jesus. He was standing patiently, listening to a man who was sarcastic with his questioning, he asked Jesus: "If you are indeed the Christ, then tell us so plainly." Jesus answered the man, "I did tell you, but you do not believe. The miracles I do in my Father's name speak for me, but you do not believe because you are not my sheep. My sheep listen to my voice, I know them and they follow me. I give them eternal life, and they shall never perish, no one can snatch them out of my hand. My Father, who has given them to me, is greater than all; no one can snatch them out of my Father's hand. I and the Father are one" (21). As some in the crowd began to rebuke Jesus, Archarius again saw the mist and he closed his eyes and waited.

Chapter 26

When Archarius opened his eyes, he was indeed back sitting on the stool outside the cells in the corner by the water barrel. Although this time, all seemed very different; his head did not ache, his mind had cleared and his eyelids were no longer heavy. His mouth was again moist, his body felt refreshed and good. He stood up and looked into the cell of Jesus. Yes, He was still there, although looking quite different from the Jesus in his visions. This Jesus was again the badly beaten man he had first met. His face was filthy, bloody with one eye now practically swollen shut. The bruises on His chest, arms and legs were forming in large black patches, only broken up by the open gashes that were choked with dried blood. Archarius could only imagine the number of broken bones that must lie under the marred skin. Not until Archarius saw Jesus in his visions did he truly noticed how badly this man had been beaten. Jesus had been beaten with vengeance and beaten with hatred to obtain the severity and number of injuries he had received on His body. Archarius remarked to himself that the true miracle was that Jesus was alive at all. He wanted to ask Jesus questions, questions that were stirred in him because of the visions he had just experienced, but he held his tongue, not wanting to disturb Jesus, concerned he might not even have the energy to respond. As Archarius started to turn, he heard Jesus say, "Come to thy shepherd so I may lead thee. I am here to teach you so you may be saved. Let us begin, for soon they will come for me."

Archarius' curiosity was so intense and his questions were so many that he immediately asked the first one. "How is it that I was able to see these visions? Was it a spell cast on me?" Jesus replied, "Is it not more important what you have heard and also the meaning than how you arrived to be there?"

Frustrated and disappointed as the visions fascinated Archarius, he knew it would be fruitless to continue asking this question. *So many things had happened in these visions, so many things did I hear*, Archarius thought, *where do I start?* His question came out of his mouth almost involuntary: "Am I one of your sheep?" He immediately felt foolish for asking such a childish question. Jesus stood and faced him and said, "Yes, my son, you are indeed one of my sheep. You know my voice and I know yours, but do you truly believe in me?" Archarius wasn't ready for that question, so he sidestepped the answer by asking another question of his. "Do I have faith?" he asked Jesus. "Faith is like a line in the sand," replied Jesus. "On one side are those who do not believe, on the other are those who are saved. Then there are those who do not even see the line or know the line exists at all.

You, Archarius, have opened your heart to see the line, but you have not yet stepped over. For that reason, I am here. For even one lost sheep saddens the Father's heart; conversely, the salvation of a single sheep is rejoiced throughout Heaven. Remember what you have seen and heard. Ask your questions, for you are very fortunate to be allowed to do so. Many will have to decide to cross the line without the benefit of what you have seen and heard." Jesus smiled as He knew Archarius' thoughts and said, "The Father knows your thoughts and knows your doubting ways, your stubbornness and your logical mind, for He created you and in you He placed those attributes; yet, you have the freedom to choose your path. Do so as you believe." "What I believe," Archarius thought out loud, "I have no idea what I believe. I have lived my whole life without this question. I have believed what I could see with my eyes and touch with my hands. I know things are what they are by the simple physical existence of the very thing I see or touch. I know of the sun, for it blinds my eyes and I can feel the heat on my skin. I know of the wind, for I can feel it and hear it and see the branches bend from its effect. I know the beasts and I know other men, for they are alive and all around me. You speak of faith which I do not know or understand, so I can only compare it to courage. Courage is just a trait of man like fear or lust. It lives in man, and it originates in man. So what is faith? Does faith live in all men? You speak of the line in the sand. What line? Who drew the line? Who cares that it exists? You say I can at least see the line. What happens if I stay where I am? What happens if I step over? What exactly is all this about and why did you choose to talk to me? These are not questions to be answered by men such as I; these are issues for men far more important than me to decide."

Jesus listened silently to Archarius ranting as he walked back and forth in front of the cell. He listened as a parent listens to a child cry about things that he does not understand. Jesus just listened, He did not answer the cries of the child. He just stood there and loved Archarius as the parent loves the frightened child. Archarius went to the water barrel and filled the mangled metal cup with water, drank quickly and suddenly threw the cup violently against the bars of Jesus' cell, water spraying into the cell and landing at the feet of Jesus. The clatter of the metal cup striking the bars echoed down the corridor. "You know I'm just a guard, not a priest! Why do you show me these things? Shouldn't you be more concerned with what awaits you in the morning? Are you in complete denial of the trouble you're in? I don't know what to think. I start to believe these things you say to me, but then I catch myself. What foolishness is this I am listening to? I am too gullible and this is what I get for not just turning a deaf ear to people like you." Archarius leaned against the wall and closed his eyes and felt the rage begin to leave him.

Archarius didn't notice, but a small tear began to mix with the blood on Jesus' face. This was the first tear to appear on Jesus's face that day. All the beatings and tauntings Jesus had endured had not caused a single tear to flow. It was the sight and sound of one of His sheep in distress that caused this Shepherd's pain.

Chapter 27

A re all decisions based on prior experiences? Do we not make any new decisions based on only the events at hand? Archarius considered these questions as he kept his eyes closed while the rage began to leave him. His head seemed always clearer after he had been angry; it was as if he cleared a dam in the river and the thoughts were no longer swirling around in his head. He was able to focus now and let the ideas and opinions enter and leave his mind until what he considered to be his true decisions remained. Why did he become so angry? Because he had been frightened as all he understood, all he had been comfortable with was brought before him and denied. New and extraordinary information had been thrown at him; is he expected to accept it without question? Forget everything he had learned and readily accept all these new ideas? Archarius remembered back to when he was a small child and in his first year of formal schooling. He remembered how he felt; the feeling was easy to recall, for it is how he felt right now. Back then at seven years old, he thought he understood the world. However, his world was only his house and his courtyard and the real world proved terrible and it frightened him. There was no one to care for him. He was alone now. He had to learn and understand everything has changed. Everything is different, his world or what he thought was his world is over and he has been thrust into a new reality. Just hours ago, he seemed comfortable for he had conquered this world. He knew the vendors on the street. He was aware of those who tricked their customers and those who were honest. He recognized the criminals that lurked in the alleys; he knew of the soldiers and the Senators that ruled the city. He understood which gods demanded worship and which gods were only slightly involved in the lives of men. He knew the seasons of the fruit trees and the patterns of the stars. He accepted that people were born and people died. He knew some men were rich and others slaves. He did not like this world he had grown up in, but he understood it and he had survived in it. He now felt as he had all those years ago as a child; he felt over-whelmed, confused, disappointed and frightened; most of all, he was frightened. All his experiences, all his judgments, all his life seemed fruitless and empty if this man is to be believed. What about his father? Had he been a fool as well? Had he been misled as well or had he misled Archarius?

Archarius stood there afraid to move, his feet as if they were standing on ice struggling to main-tain their tread. He felt so unsure about every-thing and anything that he didn't want to move or focus, for he knew not what to believe. He wanted to cry just like that seven year old boy. He wanted to rewind time and go back to before his world had been denied. Yet, the man in him understood it was all gone and it would never ever be the same again. *Wait,* he thought, *is this feeling the beginning of believing?* If his gut is telling him that all he knew and all he had understood was gone forever, did that mean he really did believe what he had just been told? Was this the faith that Jesus spoke of or is this just his acceptance of the inevitable? Would he ever even know the answer to that question? Would he be sentenced to a life of doubt and uncertainty or would the faith replace the doubt? *Everything is gone,* he said again to himself. *Would this new world be a better place than this present one which held so much promise only to turn out to be so hard and so full of tragedy and pain?*

As a boy, he heard stories of glory and stories of wonder, but he experienced little of either. Instead, he had seen hatred, jealousy and war. The only glory and awe he experienced had been in the things that had nothing to do with man. It was the land with its beautiful elements and the sea so full of mystery and the night sky which always left him in awe, no matter how old he became. The one thing he had learned was that the parts of life created by men were ugly and those not created by men were beautiful. It was those things of beauty that comprised the world he had dreamed of and hoped would one day be his reality. He rubbed his forehead until the skin began to hurt as he felt himself torn between his reality and the new reality now before him. Archarius opened his eyes and looked over at Jesus who was still standing by the bars watching him as a mother looks at her child who had just skinned his knee. His eyes seem to say, "Everything will be all right. I am here with you."

Archarius slowly shook his head. Never in his life had he been so conflicted. Jesus spoke and His words stunned Archarius: "You proclaim an appreciation for the beauty of the stars at night. When you look up at the sky, Archarius, tell me you truly believe that man knows everything of the heavens and that the gods he created are responsible for the awe you feel when you stare up into the night. There is only the Father that looks down upon the earth, caring for it as a farmer cares for his fields and how much more does He care for the children with whom He had entrusted this beautiful garden. All that you knew is not gone; it has been given reason and that reason is the Father. You were created to bring glory to the Father. You, your family, your friends, all men were created to bring glory to the Father. Do not confuse this with the earthly servants of your emperor. No, the Father creates man and gives him free will so man will glorify the Father every time he chooses love over self, puts his brother first and himself last and shares his salvation with others so they too may be saved. These acts of free will are what glorify the Father. Do not look so frightened. I know your heart as I know the heart of all men. This has been given to me by the Father so that I may bring His words to His children. I have shown you the line in the sand, Archarius; the rest is up to you. To answer your questions, yes I know what awaits me tomorrow; I have not forgotten. You see, dear Archarius, tomorrow must happen so you and all men may have a life with the Father. Once you cross that line and commit to the Father, you need to understand I am the only door to His kingdom. My sacrifice will not only create the door to my Father's kingdom, it will hold the door open forever for all men until the end of time. Man cannot leave his world and enter my Father's kingdom without the door my life will provide for them. In my name will millions of men reach eternal truth and peace. In my name will millions of men bring glory to the Father by choosing to join Him in His kingdom which is so glorious it will make the stars of the night appear as dust in the air. Sit, my dear friend, and refresh yourself with the cool water that even you have noted is better tasting than any water you have ever tasted before. Refresh yourself while I share the words of the Father with you so you can willingly step over that line and begin a new life in the Father. Now as you have seen the truth and you have proof I am not the crazy fool you alluded to in your moment of weakness, ask me what your mind must so that your heart will be released to its desires."

Chapter 28

The irony of the situation had not been lost on Archarius. He, a Roman soldier, is now the student, and the beaten and imprisoned Jesus is now officially the teacher. The problem was with every question that Archarius asked, it seemed to release a flood of more questions, most of which remain unanswered in his mind. Archarius fell back into his old logical traps as he started questioning Jesus. "If you know my heart, why do I need to ask you questions? Why can't you just tell me what I wish to know?" Jesus smiled patiently and replied, "It is as I have already told you; your free will is your path to the door of the kingdom. You need to ask, to consider, and to find your own way. That is what will bring glory to the Father." "Why does He want us to come to Him?" asked Archarius. Jesus replied, "Because He created you, all of man are His children and like any Father, He wants only the best for His children."

Again Archarius stepped back into his role of looking at everything in an orderly manner, "You talk of the Father, but you also talk of yourself. Do you both run His kingdom? Are there any other sons?" Jesus spoke slowly, "This will be difficult for you to understand and some of it you will need to rely on faith. There are three that rule the kingdom, the Father, the Son and the Holy Spirit. The Father I have told you of and the Son you see before you. The Holy Spirit will be my gift to you, once I return to the Father. The Holy Spirit will be given to those who believe and those who have faith. It will console you, support you and lead you as you exercise your free will to journey on the path to the kingdom. Things, though, are not as you can understand for these things are above you as an architect's diagrams are above an infant. The Father, the Son and the Holy Spirit are one, yet they are separate. This you will not understand but must have faith in that it is true. You must listen and trust me and soon also to listen to the Spirit as a child listens to its parent when they teach what is good and what is bad. What you may now consider to be good or bad is based on your laws as a man. You must now learn the laws of God to live a righteous life." "Are these laws you speak of, the laws of the Jews who preach in Rome?" asked Archarius. "No," replied Jesus, "these are the laws of the one true God. These are the laws that I have laid out to my followers. The covenants of the Jews have been fulfilled. The new laws are those I have given and are the only laws man will have until he resides in the kingdom of God. Other laws or manmade variations of the laws I gave you are blasphemous and are to be ignored. Beware of those who say they speak for me, for they do not have the authority and will bring pain and eternal death to those who follow them." Archarius considered all he had heard and then asked, "So if I follow the laws you say, then I am to be accepted into this kingdom?" "No, you will not," Jesus replied, "for if you did a thousand good things each day, that would not gain you even one step into the kingdom. There is only one way to enter into the kingdom and that is through your belief in me, in your faith that I am the Son of God, the only one and true God."

"Even evil men who believe in you will be allowed to enter this kingdom?" Jesus looked at Archarius as a teacher looks at a student, trying to think of how to phrase a topic so that the student will finally understand. Then Jesus replied, "Archarius, are you a citizen of Rome?" "Yes, of course," Archarius replied. Jesus continued, "Are there murderers in Rome?" "Yes," Archarius said. Jesus replied, "Are they also still citizens of Rome?" Again, Archarius answered yes. "It is similar in my Father's kingdom. All those who believe in me are citizens of my Father's kingdom; each will stand and be judged before God for his actions here in this life. Your faith in me allows you entry to the kingdom; your behavior here will dictate your judgment in heaven. Remember, though, a true believer will seek to mimic the life I have led. He will prove his faith by following my examples; he will share the message with non-believers and strive to strengthen the faith of those who already believe. Your journey on the path to the Father will be your personal history, a history that will be revealed to all and judged only by the Father. His judgment will dictate your place in the kingdom."

Archarius slipped back once more and with this question, he slipped even farther away. "But what if you're wrong? What if everyone else is right?" "Oh my dear Archarius, how you swing back and forth like a child's swing," replied Jesus. "Your faith takes root and your fears stomp out its life. There is no "if", my dear friend, for the Father and I existed long before man and all this has been foreseen. The end of days will come. This world as you know it will end and all glory will be the Father's. There is no right or wrong, no winning side and losing side; there is only what is. Your only choice, and this choice is a gift from God, is where will you stand when that day arrives."

Archarius paused as he considered all these things Jesus had told him and asked, "You say you and God have always been here; how long or how old is God?" Jesus smiled again patiently, "There is no number that can be put on forever and always. You cannot comprehend, so do not allow it to cloud your faith. God lives not in your world with its day and night and today and tomorrow. God is in the future and He is in the past as well as the present and all at the same time. This cannot be calculated as you would like it to be, so do not attempt to do so." "Is God only to judge Romans and other civilized men?" asked Archarius. "Surely he cannot allow the barbarians like those in the north into his kingdom. I understand your analogy regarding the citizens, but surely not the crazed and brutal beasts that share only the appearance of man. These bloodthirsty savages know not of your words nor would they even pause to listen, for they kill what they do not understand." Jesus seemed to smile, if only for a moment, then replied, "Are these savages, as you call them, who kill what they don't understand that different from those who plan my death tomorrow? Worry not how God will judge others, for if anything, you should dedicate your life to saving theirs by spreading the word of God. For the man who saves but one soul shall be held in more esteem in the kingdom of God than the most powerful ruler of Rome." Archarius asked, "You mention your death again; why is that necessary? Why is your task so extreme?"

Jesus looked more seriously at Archarius as he said, "Do not think for a moment that I do not anguish over this sacrifice, for I have been made man by the Father to atone for all men. For you see, man has failed. God created man and gave him his will and this earth. Yet man chose poorly. He sought the easiest path and stole and lied to his brother. He cheated and killed his brother, all to improve his position in this world. Man turned his back on the One who created him. For that reason, all of man is convicted and the judgment is harsh. God, though, so loves man that He chose to send His only Son down to earth to sacrifice His life to atone for all the sins of man and provide the doorway into the kingdom of God. All man needs to do is to accept this grace and acknowledge this gift and they will be held in the hand of God for all of eternity. God demands a penalty for man's sins, but He so loves you that He is willing to pay the penalty Himself by sacrificing His Son. The grace of this sacrifice allows yet one more gift and those are the words I have brought to man while here with you. These words are to plant the seeds of faith so that present and future generations will grow in faith and that they shall live for the glory of God. Archarius, my life, this sacrifice, even this very conversation between you and me was planned long ago, before any of this city or even this land existed.

"Now go one last time to the water barrel and drink your fill. The cool water will refresh your body and your mind and nourish the roots of faith of which I have planted in you. I must now pray to the Father, for the time of my sacrifice draws near. We will talk only once more, Archarius, and you will need to choose your faith. Will it be of men and of this world or will it be to begin on your journey to the door of heaven and give glory to God?"

Chapter 29

Archarius watched as Jesus, with great difficulty, forced Himself to kneel in the center of
the cell and now with both His eyes closed as one
had already swollen shut, began to pray to His
Father *or is it to our Father?* considered Archarius.
He wasn't thirsty and didn't want the water Jesus
had suggested he drink.

For a moment, Archarius thought facetiously
of the decision before him. *So here I am, on
what I thought would be just another day apparently deciding my eternity.* That, however, would
have been the Archarius of yesterday, for he knew
he is now a changed man, for good or bad could
be debated, but he would no longer be the man he
had been just hours ago. He had heard of others
having visions, so what he saw in his visions
did not decide the matter for him. He had also
heard of men who could stir feelings in people
like Jesus had done with him. He had also heard
of men who could perform magic, so that also
would not be a deciding factor. The odd thing is
one common attribute that is shared by all those
men, but did not seem to appear in Jesus at all
and that is self-interest. The generals who saw

visions of future battles and their subsequent victories were always the glorified victor in their visions. The men who could rally a crowd from indecision to one unified purpose were usually the one benefitting from that purpose and the men who performed magic used their power to create fear among those who watched so their magic could be used against their audience, if they were to cross them. Yes, they were all men with power who sought to better their position and increase their power over others. This Jesus, if not proved insane, has apparently allowed Himself to be arrested, severely beaten and likely to be executed without even attempting to put up a defense or arrange an escape. His reasons were that His death will excuse countless others from an eternal judgment from His Father who reigns over a kingdom Archarius had never heard of. If Archarius hadn't actually met and spoken with Jesus, he truly would have laughed off his claims and been glad that Rome would soon be rid of one more insanity case. However, he had heard Jesus and he had seen the visions and he had tasted the water from the barrel which provided the physical proof that one aspect of Archarius' logical mind sorely needed.

Archarius remembered the lessons he learned as a child, the lessons about sharing, helping, generosity and sacrifice. He had forgotten most of those lessons, for the world seemed not to care for those as much as it did for profit, pleasure and self-preservation. This is how Jesus made him feel, like an innocent child who needed to be taught the right way to live. It is such a soothing feeling to speak with Jesus; the noise and the din of the world seem to be muffled during that time. Archarius again became the wide eyed youngster eager to hear words that even at a young age, he knew were good, fair and honest words. He wished he had met Jesus outside of this prison and in better circumstances so he could continue to ask questions and to listen to Jesus answer the confusion with honest simplicity. Archarius went back to the stool and sat, his mouth was in- deed dry, so he reached for a cup of water, hoping to realize both its physical and spiritual refreshment. He dipped the battered metal cup he had drunk out of so many times before and took a very long drink. The water was again tepid and rank and it tasted foul. Gone was the cool and delicious water that he had enjoyed, gone was the feeling that came over him when he drank of the water in Jesus' presence. *Why?* he wondered. *What had turned it back to its previous condition and why?*

Archarius looked at Jesus who knelt still praying and remembered His last words when He instructed Archarius to go and drink long of the refreshing water. Archarius had declined to drink; he had declined the offer of water from Jesus and now it was gone. Would this be like Jesus' words as well? If he chose not to listen and turned away from the invitation Jesus had offered him, would it also be gone once Jesus had left? So must he make up his mind now, tonight, and this very instant? Is he to be forced to decide if everything he had been taught and everything he believed in had been wrong and everything this beaten and imprisoned man preached was right? If he did not, then would all be lost? He needed to ask Jesus this question. He needed more time. He wanted to think on this before he chose, and certainly that is what wise men would choose to do. Yes, more time to think, perhaps to gain the advice of friends or even from his family. He shouted out to Jesus, "I can't decide now; this is just too much to think about, you can't really expect me to decide something this important on the spot, can you"? The questions seemed to fall on deaf ears; Jesus neither acknowledged nor even appeared to hear him. He seemed to be in a trance, so Archarius decided to give up trying to speak to Him. Archarius knew very well in his heart his decision must be made now and also that it was expected of him now. He thought of his own situation. Yes, it would feel right to join this man and it certainly would make Jesus happy, but tomorrow, Jesus would likely be dead and where would that leave Archarius? He would be mocked and thrown out of his unit; his family would be ashamed of him and likely shun him rather than suffer in the ridicule themselves. He became bitter, thinking how his family would react and how they would abandon him out of fear. Although if the roles were reversed, would he had understood their decision without the knowledge that he had gained tonight? It was doubtful, he conceded, that he would have understood. He also admitted to himself that he would definitely be on his own if he chose to step over that line in the sand.

Archarius heard the noises in the streets above the prison. He sensed morning approaching, for he could hear the streets begin to roar to life. The wheels of the many wagons loaded down with goods to sell in the forum that morning echoed through the halls. He could hear the calls of the drivers as they drove their beasts on through the narrow streets. Rome is such a noisy city, for the buildings were all so closely built that all one had to do was listen and he could determine the time of day, who worked nearby and what they were doing. He suddenly stopped himself from this narrative as he recognized it as avoidance to the issue at hand. The sun began to rise and with the dawn would come the death of another Son, according to Jesus, the Son of God. So much to consider, one God, many gods, a man, a son of God, magicians and this Holy Spirit. Yet, one was likely true and the other a lie and falsehood, a plague upon man so that they may believe in something. It was a crutch for the weak, an argument for the learned, and a profession for the priests. But which one?! Why was he thrust into this mess, this insanity? Why did it involve him at all? Jesus had said so many things Archarius couldn't remember which ones he heard and which ones he saw in visions. *What good are His words if I can't remember them?* Where would he be when Jesus is dead and his words were forgotten? What then of His sacrifice...?

It was at that moment Archarius crossed the line in the sand. It was the moment that he realized if Jesus died and man did not carry on His message, His sacrifice would be for nothing. It was at that moment Archarius bent over and picked of the flag of Christianity from the dead hand of Jesus and spurred his own army on to spread the word through the ages. He saw this all as if it happened right in front of him. He saw himself cross the line in the sand. He knew not how he had made the decision; yet he knew that he had indeed made it. He was a Christian because he cared for Jesus' message, not because he felt the waste of Jesus dying without believers, but that he wanted to be one of the believers left behind to carry on in His place. He felt scared and cold, he felt sick to his stomach, his hands were shaking and his eyes were watering. So many things made sense at once that he couldn't process it all. He understood why honesty and integrity meant something; he understood why mercy and kindness were the way and not intimidation or force. He saw the logic in caring for the poor and helping the sick and teaching the young; he understood it all and the understanding frightened him more than any opposing army had ever frightened him on the battlefield. Yet, he was brave, for bravery is not those who are not afraid, but it stands for those who are terrified and proceed anyway because they know they must do so. This is his decision; he must proceed because he simply must. He was still shaking and his eyes were moist when he turned to look at Jesus in the cell. Again, he thought himself on the verge of insanity, for Jesus stood there looking like He had in the visions, His clothes were clean, His face no longer battered, His swollen eye open and He was standing, smiling, with one hand stretched out to him.

Chapter 30

Archarius stood and slowly walked to the cell and through the bars grasped the hand of Jesus for the first time. He wanted to speak and tell Jesus everything that he had been experiencing; all the thoughts that were swirling around in his head. The actions of his past and what decisions were right and what were wrong. For the line was clear between right and wrong now. Archarius not only saw the line in the sand; he stepped over it.

He started to speak and all that came out were the words, "I believe in you." Jesus grasped his hand firmly and said softly, "Archarius, welcome home, my son." Archarius looked into Jesus' eyes and all his shakiness left him. His body felt warm as if a wonderfully warm robe was being wrapped tightly around him. Archarius knew what he wanted now and of this he asked Jesus, "When I was small and I was with my father, we saw men by the river and there seemed to be a ceremony of sorts and I know now that you were there." Before he could go any farther, Jesus said to him, "Archarius, go to the water barrel one last time and get the cup, fill it and bring it here to me." Archarius let go reluctantly of Jesus' hand for as he did so, he felt the warm security of the robe being pulled away. He walked to the barrel and picked up the mangled metal cup that he had thrown at Jesus' feet just hours before. As he remembered this, he started to feel ashamed but Jesus said, "Think not on the past but only on the future, one that you will share with me and the Father." Archarius dipped the cup in the barrel and filled it with the water. He turned back and knelt before Jesus on the other side of the cell bars on the dirty stone tiles in the filthy hollows of the Roman building and closed his eyes. Jesus reached His hand through the bars and took the cup of water from Archarius and lifted it high above his bowed head. Jesus poured the water slowly over Archarius' head as he said, "Father, forgive this child of his sins. Bless him with the water of this cup. Place the Holy Spirit forever in his heart, carry his burdens when they exceed his strength, lead him back to the pasture when he begins to stray and count him as a child of God forever and ever." With those words, Jesus welcomed Archarius in a new family, one of which he would not nor could not ever leave.

Chapter 31

In the late morning, as Archarius stood off to the side leaning against a column, he was positioned not more than thirty yards from the court where Jesus stood motionless and appeared to be in worse shape (if that were possible) than the night before. Evidently, there were additional beatings along the way to Jesus' meeting with Pilate. The crowd had been growing increasingly ugly and the feeling that an underlying agenda had been put in place by the crowd's organizers seemed obvious to Archarius. TheJewish leaders desperately wanted Jesus out of the way, but Archarius failed to grasp why they were so threatened by Him; nevertheless, they made it a point to stir up the crowd whenever it began to subside in the least.

It seemed to Archarius that Pilate didn't agree with the seriousness of the issue, as well as he actually appeared to pity Jesus. More than once he had implored the crowd to just let the charges be satisfied with the beatings already incurred, but the crowd would only chant back angrily to crucify Him. *Crucifixion,* thought Archarius, *an odd sentence for Jesus, as He was considered to*

be a political prisoner and crucifixion was usually reserved for the worst of society. Archarius
sadly doubted Jesus would live much longer, so
he thought the sentence was moot anyway. The
scene playing out in front of him greatly troubled Archarius, for he believed in Jesus now and
although Jesus Himself had warned him this
must happen to provide atonement for mankind,
Archarius remained torn. He wanted to arrange
an escape for Jesus and return Him to His followers. Somehow, though, he knew that Jesus
would be disappointed in him if he tried to rescue
Him and would probably question his faith if he
did so. Reluctantly, he remained silent, angered
and sickened by the mob's behavior and what torture he knew would soon be inflicted on his friend.
Under pressure from the mob, Pilate finally gave
in to the surging crowd and washed his hands
of the whole mess and Jesus' fate became sealed.
Archarius winced as he saw the guards come and
take Jesus away, pushing and striking Him as He
walked. Archarius began to pray for the first time,
ironically for God to provide Jesus with a quick
death so His sacrifice would be complete and the
pain and torture would end. Tragically, this was
not to be, for Jesus was made to carry or
more literally drag the very cross He would be
crucified on through the streets and up to the
hill of Golgotha. Archarius followed along with
the mob, observing both the blood-thirsty spec-
tators as well as the silently grieving followers
of Jesus mixed in the crowds that lined both
sides of the road.

Rome did enjoy a crucifixion. *What a horrible
people we are*, Archarius thought as he witnessed

the jeering, laughing and morbid fascination with which people enjoyed the spectacle. Finally and mercifully, the guards tired of the painfully slow pace and the constant stumbling of Jesus and they chose a bystander and ordered him to assist in dragging the cross and, it seemed, Jesus as well for the final part of the journey.

Unable to stomach any more, Archarius walked away from the disgusting scene, for he did not trust himself not to intervene and he knew Jesus' time on this earth had to be very short. Archarius slowly returned home so that he might rest before his next shift in the dungeons. His mind was busy contemplating all that he had seen and heard the night before when he unconsciously spoke out loud. "So now what? What does one do who believes in the Christ?" The voice which answered his question so startled him that he drew in a sharp breath and reached for his sword as he looked around for the person who spoke the answer to his question but saw no one was near him. Archarius soon began to realize the words he had heard were just in his mind. As he considered these words, he had heard he remembered the words of Jesus, "One of the gifts that I leave you is the Holy Spirit which will help you and guide you once I am gone." With this revelation, Archarius suddenly felt the loss of Jesus and wept, for he knew Jesus must now be dead. Although relieved that the pain had mercifully ended for Jesus, he thought back to the warmth he experienced when Jesus was near to him and Archarius longed for His companionship again. The Holy Spirit, though, was indeed in him as Jesus had promised and his question was answered and Archarius now knew what he would do for the rest of his life. He slowly repeated the words out loud that the Holy Spirit had spoken to him, "Go now and save others as I have saved you, for all of heaven will rejoice for each lamb that you bring to the kingdom of God." Archarius smiled and his sandals seemed to glide upon the road.

1. Matthew 21:22
2. John 6:35
3. 1st Thessalonians 5:18
4. Luke 24:7
5. Hebrews 13:5
6. Mark 1:15
7. Isaiah 55:9
8. Luke 4:18-19
9. Deuteronomy 4:39
10. Luke 6:48-49
11. Luke 8:5-8
12. Matthew 5:3-10
13. Luke 2:11-12
14. Matthew 3:17
15. Matthew 6:25-34
16. Luke 12:32-34
17. Luke 18:9-14
18. Luke 18:16-17
19. Luke 17:22-35
20. John 10:7-18
21. John 10:25-30

CPSIA information can be obtained at www.ICGtesting.com
Printed in the USA
LVOW081130130512

281505LV00003B/7/P